PROCLAMATION COMMENTARIES

The New Testament Witnesses for Preaching   Gerhard Krodel, *Editor*

HEBREWS·JAMES· 1 and 2 PETER·JUDE· REVELATION

Reginald H. Fuller

Gerard S. Sloyan

Gerhard Krodel

Frederick W. Danker

Elisabeth Schüssler Fiorenza

FORTRESS PRESS   Philadelphia, Pennsylvania

COPYRIGHT © 1977 BY FORTRESS PRESS

Second Printing 1981

Library of Congress Catalog Card Number 76-007864
ISBN 0-8006-0584-5

9104D81   Printed in the United States of America   1-584

CONTENTS

EDITOR'S FOREWORD — v

THE LETTER TO THE HEBREWS — 1
  Reginald H. Fuller

THE LETTER OF JAMES — 28
  Gerard S. Sloyan

THE FIRST LETTER OF PETER — 50
  Gerhard Krodel

THE SECOND LETTER OF PETER — 81
  Frederick W. Danker

THE LETTER OF JUDE — 92
  Gerhard Krodel

THE REVELATION TO JOHN — 99
  Elisabeth Schüssler Fiorenza

SELECTED BIBLIOGRAPHIES — 121

EDITOR'S FOREWORD

Of the six New Testament writings discussed in this book only Revelation bears the name of its true author, John, the Christian prophet exiled on the island of Patmos. He is to be distinguished from the author of the Gospel which also bears that name. Hebrews is an anonymous writing which was eventually accepted as a letter of Paul, though the Western church rejected its Pauline authorship for centuries. Two letters, James and Jude, bear the names of brothers of Jesus, and two claim to be written by Peter, but their pseudonymity has long been recognized.

Each of the six writings contains some epistolary features, yet none of them is a genuine letter. Hebrews probably was a sermon or a series of sermons to which its author added chapter 13 before sending it off to another congregation. James is hardly a letter but rather a collection of moral maxims interspersed with phrases of direct address and preceded by a prescript. The main section of 1 Peter appears to have been a homily to recently baptized converts rather than a baptismal liturgy or a composite epistle. Jude is an anti-heretical tract addressed to all Christians. Second Peter claims to be Peter's testament in the form of an epistle with Hellenistic decreetal features. And the Revelation of Jesus Christ to John is an apocalypse with a thin epistolary frame in 1:4.

Their interpreters, like the writings themselves, belong to different traditions and have diverse backgrounds. Reginald H. Fuller teaches at the Protestant Episcopal Theological Seminary in Virginia, grew up in the Church of England and was ordained a priest of that church. Elisabeth Schüssler Fiorenza, Professor of New Testament at Notre Dame University, and Father Gerard S. Sloyan, Professor of New Testament Thought at Temple University, are both Roman Catholics. Frederick W. Danker of Concordia Seminary in Exile and I belong to two different Lutheran church bodies.

In the common endeavor to understand and interpret the diverse witness of the New Testament, scholarship manifests an aspect of the unity and catholicity of the church. It is our hope that the diverse writings interpreted in the following chapters may serve a hermeneutical function and shed light upon problems with which the contemporary proclaimer has to deal, such as spiritual lethargy (Hebrews), riches and poverty (James), pious mouthing without good works as well as liberty turning into license (James, 1 Peter), and the flight into individualistic piety without commitment to manifest Christ's Lordship in social structures (1 Peter). The theme of religion and politics is illuminated by Revelation, a crisis of authority is faced in 2 Peter, and denunciation becomes the mode and the problem of proclamation in Jude. These six writings testify in one way or another to the contradiction experienced by believers between Sunday's confession of faith and Monday's harsh realities of life, to the powerlessness experienced by believers in the face of anti-Christian forces which challenge Christ's Lordship over the world and salvation through him. While these New Testament writings do not solve our problems, they certainly contain untapped resources that can help us gain new perspectives and renew commitments.

GERHARD KRODEL
Reformation Day 1976
The Lutheran Theological Seminary at Philadelphia

THE LETTER TO THE HEBREWS

INTRODUCTION

The King James Bible entitles our document, "The Epistle of Paul the Apostle to the Hebrews." Unfortunately, every one of these claims is questioned or refuted by modern scholarship. Our document is not an epistle, it is not by Paul, it is not by an apostle, nor can it be said without qualification that it was written to the Hebrews.

Hebrews does not begin like an NT epistle. There is no opening formula such as "A to B, greetings." Instead, Hebrews plunges straight into its theological discussion with a formula recalling the prologue of John: "In many and various ways God spoke of old . . . in these last days he has spoken to us by a Son" (1:1–2). There is no thanksgiving for the recipients' progress in Christian faith and life as there is in Paul's letters, with the notable exception of Galatians. After the opening christological formula the author develops an argument about the superiority of Christ over the angels with a string of OT quotations. As we read the first chapter, the impression we get is that Hebrews is not a letter, but a theological treatise. Treatises, however, tend to be abstract, not geared to a specific situation like a letter. As soon as we begin chapter two we find the author has a very specific situation in view: "We must pay the closer attention to what we have heard, lest we drift away from it" (2:1). All through the document we find christological exposition preceded or followed by very concrete exhortation. These exhortations clearly have in mind a very specific community, or more likely a close-knit group within a larger community. But at the end we are in for another surprise. Although Hebrews does not begin like a letter, it ends like one, with personal notices, greetings, and blessings. No wonder some have thought that the epistolary conclusion was added by a later hand to dress up a treatise like a letter, while others have thought our document originally had an epistolary beginning which was cut off later. But there is no manuscript evidence for either view. Hebrews is a literary anomaly, the opposite of James, which begins like a letter but does not end like one. And both documents differ from 1 John, which neither begins nor ends like a letter.

What then is the literary form of our document? The constant alternation between christological argument and practical exhortation, and the fact that the christological argument almost invariably takes the form of an extended exposition of an OT text (e.g., Ps. 95:7–11 in Heb. 3:7–4:11), suggests that our document originated as a sermon or a course of sermons. This seems to be clinched by the reference in chapter 13 to what has gone before as a "word of exhortation" (*logos tēs paraklēseōs*). *Paraklesis* is almost a technical term for pastoral preaching as opposed to evangelism (*kerygma*) and baptismal instruction (*didachē*, *didaskalia*, or *katechēsis*). Moreover, the author refers to himself several times as "speaking" rather than writing (2:5; 8:1; 9:5). Perhaps 13:20–21 is the doxology at the end of the sermon, although this is less likely since, as we shall see, the whole of chapter 13 is probably a later appendage. If we are right in thinking that our document was originally designed as a sermon, how are we to explain the epistolary conclusion? Is it a not too successful attempt to dress up our document to make it look like a Pauline letter (M. Enslin, G. Buchanan)? If so, the ending would be as fictitious as the Pastorals, with their personal elements of a Pauline character. But that only shows the difference, for we would have expected to have an epistolary beginning as well. So with most recent commentators we take the epistolary conclusion to be genuine. What then was the author's connection with Timothy? We will take up that point a little later when we consider the document's date.

Generally speaking, the ancient Eastern church accepted Hebrews as a letter of Paul. A notable exception was Alexandria. The West, however, for a long time rejected the Pauline authorship of Hebrews, not from scholarly doubt or historical evidence, but because it did not like some of its teachings. It was especially uncomfortable with the denial of a second repentance, a point which we will pick up later. This denial was particularly awkward for the Western church when it was fighting against the Novatianists and Donatists. These heretics wished to exclude permanently all who had apostatized in time of persecution. More interesting, however, is the objection of the Alexandrian scholars. Trained in the classical tradition of literary criticism, they could not believe that Hebrews was by Paul. Its style and content were too different. Hebrews contains some of the best Greek in the New Testament, equalled only by that of the author of Luke–Acts when he has a free hand, untrammeled by the use of sources. As for content, the great Pauline themes are significantly absent, e.g., justification by grace alone through faith, or the church as the body of Christ Pauline categories such as faith are used in a very different sense. Although the kerygma of both Hebrews and Paul is centered upon the cross, Paul's theology derives its imagery from the law courts and salvation history (righteousness, justification), whereas the imagery of Hebrews is drawn chiefly from the Levitical cultus, the Day of Atonement. We cannot do better than to stick by Origen's scholarly verdict, "Who wrote it, God knows."

Attempts have been made in antiquity, at the Reformation, and in modern scholarly discussion, to find some other well-known author of the apostolic age for Hebrews. Thus Tertullian suggested Barnabas; Luther and T. W. Manson proposed Apollos, a rather more plausible hypothesis. Even Luke has been considered. The mention of Timothy in the epistolary conclusion seemed to support such theories. But clear indications that the recipients belonged to the second or third Christian generation rule out such attempts. Heb. 2:3 provides unmistakable evidence that both author and recipients belonged to the sub-apostolic age, like the author of Luke 1:1–4. There was first the period of Jesus' earthly life, then the time of the original witnesses, and finally the age of the author and recipients. Heb. 13:7 provides another pointer for the sub-apostolic date: the original leaders, who brought the gospel to the recipients, have since died.

Another factor which used to play a major role in determining the date of the document (e.g., B. F. Westcott) and which is revived from time to time (T. W. Manson, W. Manson, G. Buchanan) is the *prima facie* assumption that the temple was still standing when the work was written. The author speaks of the Levitical high priests performing their services in the sanctuary in the present tense. If this argument were tenable, it would presuppose a date before A.D. 70, although there is some possibility that sacrifices continued on the site of the temple between A.D. 70 and 135. The trouble with this argument is that the author is expounding Scripture. He is speaking of what the priests do in the Book of Leviticus, not of what was going on in the temple. The sanctuary he refers to is the tent in the wilderness, not the temple at Jerusalem.

A more sophisticated attempt to date Hebrews earlier than 70 has been made recently by G. W. Buchanan. He believes that the recipients were Christian Zionists who had literally come to Zion, the heavenly city, before its destruction (12:22–23). For the moment we simply note this view and will deal with it more fully later. Heb. 13:10 does, however, seem to speak of current priestly activities on the Day of the Atonement, rather than of the temple in the wilderness. But the argument may still be a theoretical one. It is unlikely that first century Jewish priests claimed admission to the Christian eucharist!

Like other authors of the sub-apostolic age, the author of Hebrews writes with a quasi-apostolic authority. Though not himself an eyewitness or an apostle, he presumes to address a local church or a group within it over the heads of the local leaders. The same thing happens in the Johannine Letters and in the Pastorals. All in all, the atmosphere in Hebrews suggests the early sub-apostolic age and the period of emergent catholicism. More of this will become evident as we proceed.

Properly speaking, "Hebrews" would be Aramaic speaking Palestinian Jews. In Buchanan's theory (see above) the recipients did live in Palestine, but they were Jews from the diaspora who had returned to the homeland. Were they actually diaspora Jews? The use of the LXX points in this direction. Most of the OT quotations come either from the LXX as we know it, or from a lost version of the text. Of course, many Gentile converts were familiar with the LXX, but the central concern for the Levitical priesthood and its sacrifices suggests a deep commitment to the LXX as verbally inspired Scripture. Nairne's view that the recipients were a group within a congregation has much to commend it. In 13:24 they are asked to greet "All the saints." They should by now have become teachers (5:11–14). They were neglecting attendance at the Christian assembly (10:25).

Can we be any more certain of the domicile of the recipients? Several considerations speak in favor of Rome. There are greetings to "those who come from Italy." The author seems to have people with him who are away from where the recipients live. Heb. 10:32–34 alludes to an earlier persecution in terms which nicely fit Tacitus' descriptions of the Neronian persecution in Rome back in the sixties (*theatrizomenoi*). The evident tension between the recipients and the larger congregation bears some similarity to the tensions in the Roman church which Paul writes about in Romans 14–15. Finally, the first writer to quote Hebrews was Clement of Rome (A.D. 96).

STRUCTURE

Ancient writers did not divide their works by chapter and verse, but had other ways of indicating their structure. The author of Hebrews uses the methods developed in Jewish Midrash. One of his favorite devices is the use of *inclusio*. The last words in the section repeat words which were used at the beginning. A good example of inclusio is 3:1–4:16, a midrash on Ps. 95:7–11. Several key words are introduced at the beginning: Jesus, high priest, and confession (3:1). The same words occur in 4:14. Two French scholars, L. Vaganay and A. Vanhoye, have worked out a structural analysis of the whole document, using the criteria of inclusio and catchwords. Here is an adaptation of their analysis:

I) 1:1–4. Introduction: the basic Christian confession or homologia.
II) 1:5–5:10. Preparation for the main argument.
  A) 1:5–2:18. Jesus' superiority over the angels.
  B) 3:1–6. Jesus' superiority over Moses.
  C) 3:7–4:16. Jesus' superiority over Joshua, including a hortatory midrash on Ps. 95:7–11.
  D) 5:1–10. Jesus' qualifications for high priesthood.
III) 5:11–10:39. Major christological exposition: Christ the high priest.
  A) 5:11–6:20. Introductory parenesis.
  B) 7:1–28. Christ's high priesthood after the order of Melchisedek.
  C) 8:1–9:28. The eschatological perfection of Christ's high priesthood.
  D) 10:1–18. The eschatological efficacy of Christ's high priestly work.
  E) 10:19–39. Concluding parenesis.

IV) 11:1–12:29. Major exhortation.
   A) 11:1–12:2. The heroes of faith.
   B) 12:3–13. Exhortation to endurance.
   C) 12:14–29. Exhortation to holiness.
V) 13:1–25. Appendix.
   A) 13:1–18. Ethical injunctions.
   B) 13:20–21. Concluding benediction.
   C) 13:22–25. Epistolary conclusion.

It is idle to ask which was the more important in the author's eyes, the christological exposition or the ethical exhortations. The two are inseparably connected. Faith must lead to conduct, and conduct must be based on faith. No doubt the author began with the situation of his audience. They were sluggish and stagnant, so they required exhortation. But a mere pep-talk was not enough. If the recipients (and the original audience, too) were to reach maturity in conduct, they must first develop a deeper insight into the confession of faith which they had made at their baptism.

THE USE OF THE OLD TESTAMENT

The original confession, reproduced in 1:1–3, also contained a reference to Christ's session at the right hand of God after the completion of his saving work. The imagery of the heavenly session was derived from the primitive use of Ps. 110:1 in kerygma and apologetic. Taking this as his starting point, the author will develop throughout his work an extended interpretation, a midrash on this psalm (Buchanan). The first verse of the psalm leads him naturally to v. 4 which speaks of the messianic king enthroned as high priest after the order of Melchisedek. Within this major midrash covering the whole of chapters 1–12, there are several minor midrashim. In 2:5–9 there is a midrash on Ps. 8:4–6. Another, as we have noted, is on Ps. 95:7–11 (3:7–4:11). There is one on Jer. 31:31–34 (8:8–13; 10:15–18), and within this midrash another on Ps. 40:6–8 (10:5–10). In the major parenesis there is a short midrash on Hab. 2:3–4 at 10:37–38 and a more extended one on Prov. 3:11–12 at 12:5–11. Typical of the midrash method is the way in which one OT passage can be interpreted with the help of others. All the minor midrashim contribute to the interpretation of the principal one, Ps. 110:1–4. We should also note Ps. 2:7, which is quoted at 1:5 and 5:5–9 to establish Christ's appointment by God as high priest. Ps

8:4–6 is used at 2:5–9 to make the point that Christ's temporary humiliation on the cross was a necessary precondition of his exaltation. Hence, his humiliation by no means implies his inferiority to the angels.

Without a direct quotation, the story of Abraham's encounter with Melchisedek (Gen. 14:17–20) is reproduced at some length in 7:1–10 to prove the superiority of the high priesthood according to Melchisedek over the Levitical. This argument is hardly likely to convince the present day reader, but it was typical of the midrashic technique. Today, we may accept the conclusion without buying the argument!

Another important text which enriches the interpretation of Psalm 110 is Jeremiah's prophecy of the new covenant. It demonstrates that the OT itself was fully aware of the ineffectiveness of the Levitical priesthood and of God's plan to replace it eventually with a better priesthood. Note here that the author regards both the covenant and the law as the institution of a priesthood. Its moral purpose or its function as a summons to repentance are completely disregarded. In chapter 9 the Levitical legislation for the Day of Atonement is summarized without direct quotation (9:7–10). Then, resuming the covenant theme, the author expands the picture by an allusion to the covenant sacrifice offered by Moses in Exod. 24:6–8. Thus we have a confusion of typologies. The author is untroubled by this. He wants to bring out two different, though related aspects of the effects of Christ's death.

Ps. 40:6–8 plays an important role in the Christology of Hebrews (10:5–10). The author calls attention to the singular reading of the LXX, "A body hast thou prepared for me." The Hebrew text has "my ears hast thou opened"—to hear God's commandments and obey his will. The whole purpose of the incarnation ("when Christ came into the world") was that he should have a body to offer in sacrifice. This would qualify him to fulfill the role of high priest after the order of Melchisedek. Once more, a subordinate text supports and amplifies the main text (Ps. 110:4).

Later the author reverts to Jeremiah's prophecy to demonstrate that under the new covenant God will "no more remember" (i.e., punish) the sins of his people (10:16–17). This proves the finality of Christ's atonement. Under the old covenant, God did remember sins, and Jeremiah looked forward to their final removal. This has now been achieved, and so there is no longer any need for atonement. Christ's priesthood is eternal, not one whose service must constantly be repeated, whether in the daily sacrifice or annually on the Day of Atonement. In the major parenesis Hab. 2:3–4, a testimonium also used at Qumran and by Paul, is cited for quite a different purpose. The Christian must hold on until the final consummation.

The last text, Prov. 3:11–12, is used (12:5–6) to assure the readers that persecution throws no doubt on the validity of their salvation. God chastises his true-born sons, so persecution is a sign that they are not illegitimate.

THE HIGH PRIESTHOOD OF CHRIST

We now come to the central doctrine of Hebrews and its signal contribution to Christology. Was the author the first to use this title? Some have thought that 3:1 ("high priest of our confession") indicates that the baptismal confession of the community already contained the title. This, however, is doubtful. The exact wording of the confession, as G. Bornkamm has shown, is to be found in 1:1–3. This culminates in the statement that when he had made purification for sins, Christ sat down at the right hand of the majesty of high. The homologia thus contained an allusion to Ps. 110:1, but not to 110:4. The earlier kerygma had used v. 1 atomistically. The author takes a new step by applying the psalm as a whole to Christ. Thus the homologia *implied* that Christ is high priest after the order of Melchisedek.

But was the substance of this Christology new? Not altogether. Quite early on, the liturgical tradition had interpreted Christ's death as a sacrifice (1 Cor. 11:24, *hyper hymōn*; Mark 14:24, *ekchynnomennon hyper pollōn*; Mark 10:45, *lytron anti pollōn*). In his own theologizing, Paul had preferred the imagery of the law court and the battlefield, though sometimes he drew on liturgical formulas which spoke of Christ's death as a sacrifice (cf. also 1 Cor. 5:7). The author of Hebrews is clearly aware of this liturgical tradition. By combining this tradition with the extension of Ps. 110:1 to v. 4 he arrived at his new doctrine.

It is also possible that the author was influenced by Jewish precedents. Long before he wrote, the Hasmonean priestly rulers had supported their pretensions by an appeal to Psalm 110. The eleventh cave of Qumran has yielded a scroll which shows that the covenanters looked for the coming of Melchisedek as a messianic figure (11Q Melch.). Philo identified the logos as a high priest. Clearly the notion of a priestly Messiah after the order of Melchisedek was, so to speak, in the air in contemporary Judaism, especially in some of its sectarian forms. There were currents of thought originating in Palestine which spread to Hellenistic Judaism, both in its Philonic form and in a Christian form in Hebrews. This will be an important point to remember when we consider the author's intellectual milieu.

The author, however, was not interested in theological speculation for its own sake. It was the situation of his readers, as evidenced in the hortatory sections, that led him to elaborate his doctrine:

> You have become dull of hearing. For though by this time you ought to be teachers, you need someone to teach you again the first principles of God's word. You need milk, not solid food (5:11–12).

Nevertheless, the writer will give them solid food: "Therefore, let us leave the elementary doctrines of Christ" (6:1). The high priesthood of Christ is a mature doctrine, a further indication, incidentally, that it was not part of the original baptismal confession. The doctrine of Christ's high priesthood would lead the readers into maturity and overcome their sluggishness and stagnation. How will it do this? The author sets up a comparison between the recipients and Israel in the wilderness. The Israelites of the exodus had also grown tired. They too had murmured, and wanted to return to the fleshpots of Egypt instead of holding on until they reached the promised land (midrash on Psalm 95 in 3:7–4:11). Like the children of Israel, the community of the new covenant lives between the times. The former lived between the bondage of Egypt and the freedom of the promised land, the latter between the first and second comings of Christ. For each interim God has provided a priesthood and a sacrificial system to enable the wanderers to enter into the promised rest. Hence it will be seen that the doctrine of Christ's high priesthood was not intended as an abstract piece of theologizing. It was a matter of life and death for the original recipients of the document.

For the same reason it was important that the sacrifice of Christ should be final. There was no place for any other. If they turned their backs on this salvation, the readers would get no second chance. There was no further sacrifice for sin. This denial of a second repentance will be discussed later in these pages.

The author expounds his new doctrine by a point by point comparison between the Levitical high priesthood and that of Christ. Why does he take this line? There is really no suggestion that the recipients were in danger of returning to the temple sacrifices. Probably the temple had been destroyed by then and the temple sacrifices were hardly a live option for them, especially if, as we think, they lived outside of Palestine. This comparison is motivated by two considerations. First, there is the author's scriptural orientation. He believes that the OT is not only the inspired word of God, but was written in direct reference to his own day. Second, there is the analogy between the wilderness generation and the church of the new covenant, as already noted.

If the whole epistle, as we have claimed, is an extended midrash on Psalm 110, this will mean that the document in its entirety is related to that text, and to the exposition of Christ's high priesthood. This is obvious in the central section (5:1–10:39), and fairly obvious in the major exhortation (11:1–12:29). It is less obvious in 1:1–4:16. But there are, to begin with, three references to Christ as high priest in these opening chapters. The first occurs in 2:17, in the section which demonstrates Christ's superiority over the angels. Has the author planted this first reference arbitrarily or does it have an integral connection with Christ's superiority over the angels? We suggest that it has. The old "message," i.e., the Mosaic law or old covenant, was "declared by angels" (2:2). This was a common notion in contemporary Judaism and it was also taken up by Paul in Gal. 3:19 and by the author of Luke–Acts in Stephen's speech (Acts 7:38, 53), but for different purposes. The author of Hebrews is concerned with the law simply and solely because it instituted the Levitical priesthood and its sacrifices. In demonstrating Christ's superiority over Moses, therefore, the author is preparing his readers for his thesis that Christ's high priesthood is superior to the Levitical. Wherever we read of angels in the first two chapters, we must conceive of their function in this way.

The second enunciation of the main theme occurs at 3:1. This is the opening verse of the section which deals with Christ's superiority over Moses. Moses is introduced as the "servant" of the house, i.e., the house of Israel (Num. 12:7). It is also said that Moses "testified to the things that were to be spoken later" (v. 5). What things are these? The usual interpretation is that they are the revelation to be brought later by Christ and his apostles (so Thomas Aquinas). However, Moses is always a negative witness in Hebrews. He represents solely the Levitical priesthood which is done away with in Christ. When the author needs prophecies of Christ and his work, he does not refer to Moses, i.e. the Pentateuch, but almost exclusively to the prophets and psalms. So the "things" of 3:5 must be the revelation of the law which Moses was soon to give according to Num. 12:8. The RSV "later" is not in the Greek text. Remove that, and put yourself at the point of time when Moses went up the mountain to receive the law and the difficulty disappears. Once more, the point of the argument is the superiority of Christ over Moses as the instituter of the old covenant and the Levitical priesthood. Hence the priesthood of Christ is superior to that which Moses instituted.

The midrash on Psalm 95 (chap. 4) focuses similarly on Christ's superiority over Joshua. The name Joshua is "Jesus" in the Greek. The first Jesus did not bring Israel into the eschatological rest but only into the earthly promised land. Only the second Jesus did that. Therefore his high priesthood is more effective than Joshua's leadership. The Joshua passage is significantly followed by the third enunciation of the main theme (4:14). This confirms that the comparison with Joshua is related to the high priesthood of Christ.

The author is now ready to tackle his subject head-on. But first he must establish what was not obvious—that Jesus had the proper qualifications to be a high priest. It was not obvious because the necessary requirements were duly set out in the Pentateuch, and only the descendants of Levi could fulfill them. Nevertheless, Jesus does fulfill the essential qualifications. The high priest must be chosen from among men for his sacred functions. He must share the weakness of those on whose behalf he functions. Only so can he sympathize with them. He must not take this honor upon himself, but must be called by God.

Jesus measured up to all these points, as is proved by a combined quotation of Psalm 2:7 and Ps. 110:1 (5:5–6). The argument is clinched by yet another enunciation of the main theme (5:10).

Before embarking on a point by point comparison between Christ and the Levitical high priests, the author inserts a long exhortation (5:11–6:20), which serves to remind the readers once more of the practical purpose of the christological exposition. It indicates that what follows is to be advanced teaching for the mature.

Skillfully, the author steers his exhortation back to the major theme by discussion of God's promise to Abraham (6:13–20). It was a promise given under oath. Hence the readers can have confidence that they will enter where Jesus has gone before, a high priest after the order of Melchisedek. This is the fifth and final enunciation of the theme.

At last we are ready for the central argument (7:1–10:18). First, there is a discussion of the story of Abraham and Melchisedek as related in Genesis 14 (7:1–10). The transition was made smooth by the previous discussion of God's oath to Abraham. The Genesis story does not mention Melchisedek's father, mother, or genealogy, nor does it say anything of his death. This suggests that he is a mysterious figure from eternity, and so he "resembles" the Son of God as a priest forever. Melchisedek is thus not a type of Christ, for types have a historical reality. Rather, he is a shadowy *Doppelgänger* of the Christ (7:1–3).

In the next section (7:4–10) we get a proof from the Genesis story that Scripture itself recognizes the superiority of Melchisedek's —and therefore Christ's—priesthood over Levi's.

Vv. 11–14 illustrate the indispensable role of Melchisedek in the argument. Ps. 110:4, written later than the Pentateuch, shows that the Levitical priesthood is not the only one. So, in spite of his descent from Judah rather than Levi, "our Lord" could nevertheless occupy a priestly office.

There are two more reasons why Christ is superior to the Levitical priests (7:15–19). His priesthood is not based on physical descent, nor on an ineffective law. The old priesthood could not achieve "perfection." Here we have a key term of Hebrews which will be discussed later.

The next point (7:20–22) is that there is no oath in connection with the appointment of the Levitical priests, but there was for the

Melchisedek priesthood. This is clear from Ps. 110:4, though it is not clear when the oath appointing Jesus was sworn. No doubt it was implied in the exaltation of Christ to the right hand of God.

There was a constant succession of Levitical priests. When one died, another took his place. Once again, it is clear that the author's argument is purely scriptural. Had he been talking of the high priests of Jerusalem of the first century A.D., he could hardly have avoided mention of their frequent deposition for political reasons! But Jesus has no successor. His tenure is permanent. Therefore he lives to make perpetual intercession for his own, that they too may gain access to the presence of God (7:23-25).

Christ, moreover, was sinless. He did not have to offer sacrifice every day for his own sins and those of others. Note how the author shifts from the Day of Atonement to the daily sacrifices. The reason is the point he is making: he wishes to emphasize the constant repetition of the Levitical ministrations. Christ's sacrifice is superior because he was offered once and for all and its effects last forever (7:26-29).

8:1-7. The scene of the ministrations of the two priesthoods is also different. The Levitical priests ministered in the tent in the wilderness; Christ performs his priestly liturgy in heaven. He could never have exercised his priesthood on earth since the office was already occupied (v. 4). The earthly sanctuary was a mere copy of the true, a point which prepares the ground for the next argument. Even the OT recognized the inadequacy of the first priesthood (v. 7).

That inadequacy was pointed up by Jeremiah's prophecy of a new covenant. There would have been no need for a new one if the old one had done its job properly (8:8-13). With evident fascination, the author enumerates every detail of the furniture in the earthly sanctuary (9:1-5). He would have loved to give a typological interpretation to every item, but unfortunately he had no time. So he focuses at once on the ritual of the earthly sanctuary (9:6-10). That ritual was ineffective because it could only deal with external breeches of the ceremonial law. It could not remove the barrier between man and God, the barrier of sin. That, however, is just what Christ's work did (vv. 11-14). He entered into the very presence of God, taking with him not the blood of animals, but his own blood.

The core of the argument is contained in these two sections, 9:6–10 and 11–14. The first paragraph describes the work and effects of the Levitical high priesthood, while the second (the central paragraph of the whole document) describes the work of Christ and *its* effects. The high priest performs his office on earth, but Christ performs his in heaven; the high priest offered the blood of animals, but Christ offered his own blood. The high priest took the blood into the earthly sanctuary, Christ took his into heaven itself. The Levitical sacrifices covered only ritual impurity, Christ's sacrifice took away sin, enabling the worshipers to serve the living God.

In 9:15–22 the theme of the two covenants reappears. The inauguration of the first covenant (and with it the Levitical priesthood) is contrasted with the death of Christ. Here again we see that the author is not concerned with the Day of Atonement *per se*, but with the saving work of Christ. While the Day of Atonement is the most helpful image, there are other images too, like the daily sacrifice which we have already encountered, and the inaugural sacrifice of the covenant at Sinai in this section. The point which the author wants to make is that covenants have to be inaugurated by a death. He reinforces the argument by a play on the word *diathēkē*, which can mean both a covenant and a will. Wills only come into force when the testator dies.

9:23–28 contains a curious argument: just as the furniture in the earthly sanctuary had to be cleansed on the Day of Atonement, so the heavenly things of which the earthly are only a copy require purification. It is not clear what the heavenly things are, or why they required purification. The author has been carried away by his argument.

10:1–4 contains no new arguments but underlines points already made: the shadowy nature of the old ritual, its ineffectiveness and need of constant repetition, the inability of animal sacrifices to take away sins. But these verses do prepare the way for something new, the introduction of Ps. 40:6–8 into the picture (10:5–10). The nature of Christ's sacrifice was an act of obedience to the will of God. This does not mean that it was a purely ethical act. The will of God for Christ was precisely that he should die as a sacrificial victim. But as we shall see later, this use of Psalm 40 does open up the possibility of a modern reinterpretation of Hebrews' central thesis.

With 10:11–18 the theological exposition is rounded off. Once more, the author contrasts the two sacrificial systems. Once more he alludes to the daily oblation, and contrasts it with the singularity of Christ's sacrifice and the finality of its effects. No more sin, no more offering. The problem of post-baptismal sin, apart from the unforgivable sin of apostasy, is simply not raised.

As our structural analysis shows, 10:19–39 concludes the christological exposition with an exhortation corresponding to the initial exhortation in 5:11–6:20. Key words from the exposition are introduced here, such as "enter," "sanctuary," "blood of Jesus," "way opened up for us through the curtain," "great high priest," "draw near," "confession." These catchwords rivet together the exposition and the parenesis and show that the latter belongs here and not to the major exhortation, which begins in 11:1.

SOME RESIDUAL THEOLOGICAL PROBLEMS

Christ's Sacrifice: at Calvary or in heaven?

Since the Reformation there has been much debate over the scene of Christ's sacrifice. Some exegetes, mainly Protestant, have tried to locate that sacrifice exclusively on the cross. In favor of this interpretation one may cite the tremendous emphasis on the once for all (*eph' hapax*) character of Christ's sacrifice and its interpretation in terms of obedience (10:7). Also, Christ's session at the right hand of God indicates the completion of his work. The verb *prosphero* invariably occurs in the aorist tense. On the other hand, many argue that the real scene of Christ's sacrifice is in heaven. It is there that he presents his blood to the Father. And this he does continuously for the atonement of our sins. The following arguments are used in support of this position: In the sacrificial system of the OT the real moment of sacrifice was not the slaying of the victim but the manipulation of the blood after it had been slain. That the author of Hebrews presumes this rationale is indicated by his curious insistence that the cult objects in the heavenly sanctuary must be cleansed by an application of the blood. Hence Christ's priesthood is eternal, and his sacrifice goes on in eternity. Those who argue for this position frequently interpret Hebrews on Platonic lines (e.g., M. Bourke). It will be noted, however, that this is only an inference and is by no means certain. The only specific activity ascribed to Christ in heaven is that of making perpetual intercession for us (Heb. 7:25), or appearing in the presence of God on our behalf (9:24). The author, as we have noted, is careful to put the words about Christ's self-offering in the aorist. There must be some reason for this.

Whatever the original understanding of sacrifice in the OT was, Hebrews clearly regards the slaughter of the victim as an essential moment in the ritual, along with the presentation of the blood in the sanctuary. Accordingly, what happened at Calvary was no mere preliminary, but an essential part of the sacrifice. That sacrifice, however, is not confined to Calvary. It includes the presentation of his blood in heaven to the Father. But this happened once and for all, not eternally. It must therefore have happened at the moment of his entry into the heavenly sanctuary. The *eph' hapax* of his self-oblation embraces the death and exaltation as a single, indivisible event. Of course, Christ continues his high priestly work in eternity, yet that work is not eternal self-oblation, but intercession and appearance before the presence of God for his own on the grounds of his once for all self-offering (7:25; 9:24). Although Hebrews does not use the term, it would probably be legitimate to say that he eternally "pleads" his once for all sacrifice.

The Contemporary Meaning of Sacrifice

There is a tendency among some scholars to write off the Christology of Hebrews as meaningless for contemporary faith so far as the doctrine of Christ's high priesthood and sacrifice are concerned. Our understanding of that Christology depends upon an experience of the sacrificial cultus which we do not have today. One is reminded of Sir Edwyn Hoskyns' once expressed desire that an ox might be sacrificed annually in the court of Corpus Christi College, Cambridge, preferably on a hot summer's afternoon. That would teach theological students what sacrifice was all about! Unfortunately it would be a curious and disgusting spectacle, rather than an existential experience.

But is such an existential experience really necessary? We do use the term sacrifice today, and we use it in a sense transformed by the sacrifice of Christ. We speak of a soldier making the supreme sacrifice for his country, an act which a popular hymn refers to as a "lesser Calvary." We speak of a mother sacrificing her life in a fire to rescue her child. The OT prophets taught that the real sacrifice God required was ethical obedience. This ethical reinterpretation of the concept made great strides in Hellenistic Judaism, and found its way into the NT (Rom. 12:1; Heb. 13:16; 1 Pet. 2:5, 9). But if God demands that kind of sacrifice, human beings are incapable of rendering it. When the prophets sought to ethicize the concept of sacrifice, they were perhaps insufficiently aware of the problem. But the very continuation, nay, elaboration of the sacrificial system in postexilic times was a witness to this impossibility (O. C. Quick). Thus the OT prophets unconsciously pointed forward to the need for God to do for humanity what it could not do for itself. This was done, according to Hebrews, by Christ, the "apostle" of God at Calvary, and in his exaltation. Hebrews does not draw its understanding of Christ's redeeming work exclusively from the obsolete sacrificial system. After all, our document was not describing a living rite of which his hearers had an existential experience, but the scriptural arrangements for the tent in the wilderness. Now, as we have seen, Hebrews also draws upon one of the psalms which encapsulates the prophetic protest against cultic sacrifice:

> Sacrifices and offerings thou hast not desired, but a body hast thou prepared for me; in burnt offerings and sin offerings thou hast taken no pleasure. Then I said, "Lo, I have come to do thy will, O God," as it is written of me in the roll of the book. (10:5–6)

Of course, as we have already said, the author did not intend to eliminate the cultic element in sacrifice. This is clear from his repeated use of the term, blood of Christ. But he does open up the possibility of interpreting Christ's sacrifice in ethical terms today. After all, sacrifice is only one of the images used to interpret the meaning of Christ's death. Matthew speaks of Christ's life in its totality as the fulfillment of all righteousness. Paul speaks of the perfect obedience of the last Adam which reversed the disobedience of the first. The cross is the climax of the total life of obedience, and acquires its significance from the quality of the life that preceded it. By that perfect obedience to the will of the Father, Christ did for humanity what it could not do for itself. God required total obedience; Christ rendered it, and Christ alone. This is the truth in the controversial, yet scriptural, doctrine of satisfaction. It is not, however, as has often been thought, an immoral doctrine, as though Christ offered the sacrifice and we can get off scot-free. It is not that since Christ has offered his sacrifice of perfect obedience we have nothing to do at all. Rather, it means that Christ has opened up the way of obedience for us. Now at last we can fulfill what the prophets demanded. Christ takes up our imperfect obedience into his perfect obedience:

> Look, Father, look on his anointed face,
>   and only look on us as found in him.

Christ in Hebrews is the pioneer, the one who went before that we might follow. Two analogies may help us to understand the relation between Christ's obedience and ours. C. S. Lewis once compared the situation to that of a child trying to make his first letters. The father puts his own large hand over the child's small hand and traces the letters with him. E. Schweizer compared the situation to an experience of his own childhood. In the alpine snows his father would walk ahead making footsteps in which the child could follow. In this way it does seem possible to make homiletical sense of a Christology which originally depended for its comprehension upon an understanding of the sacrificial cultus which we no longer share.

Other Aspects of Hebrews' Christology

While the high priesthood of Christ forms the central concept of Hebrews' Christology and its original contribution, there are other titles and concepts as well. The opening hymn uses the title Son of God to cover the three stages of preexistence, earthly life, and exaltation. The preexistence part of the formula is based upon the concept of the heavenly wisdom, similar to that found in other hymnic formulae (Phil. 2:6–11; Col. 1:15–20; John 1:1–18). Unless the reading *huios* (Son) is original at John 1:18, the Hebrews formula is the only one which directly identifies the preexistent one with the Son.

The author never makes it quite clear where he locates the moment at which the preexistent Son became incarnate. One would naturally think, of course, of the birth or conception and this certainly seems to be suggested by 1:6, especially when it is read as the liturgical Epistle on Christmas Day. However, this is probably not the author's meaning. The quotation from Deut. 32:43 (LXX) is framed by two other OT quotations which refer to the enthronement of Jesus at the exaltation (Psalm 2:7 in v. 5 and 45:6–7 in vv. 8–9). Accordingly it seems best to take "into the world" as a translation of *le' olam*. In this passage the term Son of God is used to express the dignity of the exalted One. We have here a combination of a three-stage Christology of the gentile mission with a more primitive two-stage Christology of Hellenistic Jewish Christianity, as in Phil. 2:6–11. As applied to the exaltation, the title Son of God acquires a special nuance in Hebrews from the high priesthood Christology. This is especially clear in 4:14 where the two titles are brought together.

Between preexistence and exaltation comes the incarnate life. As has often been noted, Hebrews lays extraordinary emphasis upon the humanity of Jesus. He shared the flesh and blood of mankind (2:14). God prepared a body for him (10:5). He assumed the seed of Abraham and became like his brethren in every respect (2:16–17). Is this a particular emphasis upon Jesus' Jewishness? Probably not, for in the context the human qualities specified are quite general, liability to temptation, suffering, and death. As a christological title, "Son of God" covers the incarnate life. Though he was a Son, Jesus learned obedience through suffering (5:8). This passage, with its emphasis on Jesus' prayer for deliverance from the terrors of death, is almost certainly based on the synoptic traditions of Gethsemane. It seems to portray Jesus as the suffering servant of Deutero-Isaiah. Thus Hebrews has a three-stage Christology, each stage of which is covered by the title, Son of God.

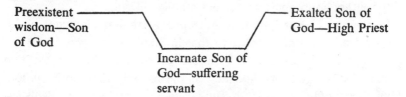

Preexistent wisdom—Son of God

Exalted Son of God—High Priest

Incarnate Son of God—suffering servant

Nothing is said of Jesus' Davidic descent, and Buchanan thinks Hebrews deliberately rejected it. This is improbable. In primitive Christology Jesus' Davidic descent was not in itself a christological concept, but a necessary qualification for the exalted messiahship. It was inappropriate for the exalted state as Mark 12:35–37 makes clear. This pericope cites Ps. 110:1, which is also the main text of Hebrews. Hebrews' attitude to the title son of David was probably the same as that of the synoptic pericope. Like it, our author probably took for granted Jesus' Davidic descent as a necessary qualification for his messiahship. But the main weight of his Christology lay upon the exaltation.

In a citation of Ps. 8:4–6 Hebrews once applies the title Son of man indirectly to Jesus in his earthly existence (2:5–8). The author of Hebrews was evidently aware of the synoptic use of Son of man as a self-designation of Jesus in his earthly activity and humiliation. This tradition enabled him to apply Psalm 8 christologically to Jesus. Son of man as a christological title for Hebrews expresses humiliation as the pathway to exaltation.

THE MAJOR EXHORTATION, 11:1–12:29

This section balances the major christological exposition. It sets forth the appropriate ethical response to Christ's saving work, and defines that response as faith. Faith for Hebrews is very different from what it was for Paul. For Paul it denoted the moment of passivity in which the believer accepts Christ's saving work as a gift from God. For Hebrews, it is a human virtue (11:1) closely related to endurance (*hypomonē*) and hope (*elpis*). Faith also involves holding fast the confession of faith, the *homologia*. Thus faith is also becoming a matter of affirming dogmatic propositions. It is *fides quae creditur* rather than *fides qua creditur*, the faith which is believed rather than the faith by which we believe. These developments (faith as virtue and as "the" faith) in the meaning of faith are signs of the author's sub-apostolic, early Catholic outlook.

In chapter 11 our author draws upon a traditional recital of Israel's salvation history similar to that in Stephen's speech (Acts 7). This need not imply a direct literary connection between the two recitals, as W. Manson thought. It means only that both authors drew their traditions from a similar milieu, probably Hellenistic–Jewish. This type of recital was developed in the wisdom literature. Earlier recitals in the OT praised Yahweh for his mighty acts. The later recitals praise the heroes of the past for their mighty deeds. Typical is the *exordium* of Sirach 44, "Let us now praise famous men." So Hebrews praises the heroes of the past for their faith. Its perspective on salvation history again suggests an early Catholic standpoint.

The first two verses of chapter 12 are a redactional link between the recital of chapter 11 and the exhortations based upon it (12:3–29). V. 2 looks like a christological hymn, and serves to join the ensuing exhortation with the major christological exposition. Note especially the reference to Christ's session at the right hand of God. This is the only occurrence of the word "cross" in Hebrews, a fact which suggests a Paulinist origin for the hymn, similar to that in Phil. 2:6–11. Jesus is the supreme hero of faith, conceived as endurance. To take the cross of Christ as an ethical example in this way is again typically sub-apostolic, and recalls 1 Pet. 2:21–25. The author wishes to exhort his readers to pursue the same virtue of faith at a time of persecution. He develops his point by means of a midrash on Prov. 3:11–12 (12:5–11). This midrash is followed by a more general exhortation to holiness (12:12–17), a requirement of all the baptized (cf. 1 Pet. 1:14–16). Once more, the imperatives are grounded on an indicative (12:18–24). The Christian assembly is compared to the gathering of the old community at Sinai which received the law. Once more, we must remember that for our author the law meant specifically the institution of the Levitical priesthood. These verses are important for the author's understanding of Christian worship (cf. also v. 28). The liturgy is an earthly foretaste of the eschatological worship in the heavenly Jerusalem. V. 24 provides another link with the major christological exposition, while vv. 25–29 offer a concluding warning.

APPENDIX:
A BRIEF CATECHESIS AND EPISTOLARY CONCLUSION

With the conclusion of chapter 12 the main body of the document is completed. Chapter 13 is an appendix. Some (e.g., Spicq, Vanhoye, and Buchanan) consider it an addition from a later hand. Buchanan believes it was added quite late and that its intention was to dress up the letter as a Pauline Epistle in order to secure its acceptance in the NT canon. But there is little in the chapter to suggest a different hand. It exhibits the same concern for Christian worship that we found in chapter 12 (see 13:10–16). The "city which is to come" (13:14) recalls the heavenly Jerusalem of 12:22. The same situation of a church faced with persecution is presupposed (13:3). True, there are some minor differences. Only chapter 13 mentions marriage (v. 4), a point Buchanan uses to support his thesis that the original document was addressed to a monastic community. That, however, is an argument from silence. 13:1–5a looks like a catechesis similar to those in the hortatory parts of other NT epistles. Note the similarity in style between this passage and Rom. 12:3–21. In both passages imperatives are expressed by nouns and adjectival complements without a copula. Another difference is that the closing benediction (13:20–21) mentions the resurrection, whereas the main part of the document speaks invariably of Christ's exaltation. This difference, however, is probably due to the use of a traditional formula.

Finally, we have a proper epistolary conclusion in vv. 22–24. "Briefly" is surprising after chapters 1–12, but it may refer simply to chapter 13 (Buchanan). If this is the case, "word of exhortation" will likewise refer only to chapter 13.

What then is the author's purpose in appending chapter 13? The most probable explanation is that he was adapting a sermon or series of sermons which he had already composed or preached, and sent it off to another congregation for whose needs he considered it to be relevant. And with it he sends a special exhortation particularly adapted to them, with a blessing and epistolary conclusion.

RESIDUAL ETHICAL PROBLEMS

Four problems call for a particular discussion. These are:

1) The meaning of "perfection" in Hebrews.
2) The sacrificial nature of Christian worship.
3) The denial of a second repentance.
4) The concept of the rest which awaits the people of God.

Perfection

This term has both christological and ethical significance. Christ achieved perfection through suffering (5:8–9), and the Christian likewise must grow toward perfection (6:1; cf. 12:2).

Perfection (*teleiōsis*) means etymologically to achieve a *telos* or goal. For the author of Hebrews it is primarily a religious and only secondarily an ethical category. As a religious term it means to attain the goal of all religion, which is access to the presence of God in worship. Christ through his self-oblation entered into the presence of God and won eternal redemption for us. His perfection or achievement of his goal was reached when he sat down at the right hand of God. As the pioneer he passed through the veil which cut us off from the presence of God and opened up for us the way to achieve the same perfection. In each case there is an ethical element involved. For Christ, this consisted in his perfect obedience to the will of God, as expounded in the midrash on Psalm 40 (10:5–10). In our case ethical perfection consists of holiness, without which none will see the Lord. It includes purity from all defilement of sin. Here as elsewhere the indicative implies an imperative.

The Sacrificial Nature of Christian Worship

No author has insisted so strongly on the once for all character of Christ's sacrifice. It was from his teaching that the Anglican Reformers composed their prayer of consecration: "Who made there by his one oblation of himself once offered, a full, perfect and sufficient sacrifice, oblation and satisfaction for the sins of the whole world." At the same time our author does speak in his appendix about a sacrifice which Christians have to offer. It is twofold. One aspect is liturgical, a sacrifice of praise: "the fruit of lips that acknowledge his name" (13:15). The other aspect is ethical: "to do good and to share what you have for such sacrifices are pleasing to God" (13:16). Our author can even say that the Christians have an altar in which they partake (13:10). He is clearly talking about a different kind of sacrifice from the salvific, atoning sacrifice of Christ. The Christian sacrifices have no atoning value. Rather, they are a *response* to the atoning sacrifice of Christ. Do these sacrifices include the eucharist?

F. F. Bruce quotes with approval Bengel's pithy comment on Heb. 13:10, *"nil de missa."* Yet surely, the sacrifice of praise is present in the eucharist, since it was preeminently at the eucharist that a confessional recital of the redemptive acts of God in Christ was presented. But, of course, this does not exclude other offerings of praise outside of the eucharist. Thus Hebrews justifies our using sacrificial language for the eucharist. The word "altar" in 13:10 may well, despite Bengel and Bruce, *also* refer to the eucharist (so Bornkamm, Michel). For in that liturgical action thanksgiving is offered for Christ's redeeming work, and that redeeming work thereby becomes a present reality. The author does not draw this deduction himself, but he may well imply it. It is not inconsistent with his teaching about the once for all character of Christ's atoning sacrifice. Hebrews is thus already developing a line of thought which was to become explicit a few years later in the Didache, where for the first time the eucharist is actually called a sacrifice. In this respect, too, Hebrews is a document of emergent Catholicism.

The Denial of a Second Repentance

One of the greatest difficulties in Hebrews is its denial of the possibility of a second repentance (6:4–6; 10:26–31 and its use of the example of Esau in 12:16–17). When the Western church was locked in combat with the Novatianists and Donatists, it refused to accept Hebrews into the canon because of this teaching and denied its Pauline authorship. The mainline church wanted to receive apostates back into the fold when persecutions were over and found the teaching of Hebrews embarrassing. How are we to interpret this teaching and what authority does it have for us today?

First, we may agree with Williamson that the author restricts his rigorism to the ultimate sin of apostasy. This is clear from the language of 6:6. He does not extend it to cover all post-baptismal sin, *contra* Buchanan, who sees here another expression of the author's monastic sectarianism.

Even so, does this mean that apostasy is for all time unforgivable? Is this a permanent law for the church? The issue becomes problematical whenever a persecution ceases. It became so in the German churches after the *Kirchenkampf*. Generally, the church has taken a compromise position. Apostates have usually been put on probation and allowed to work their passage home. But is this consistent with the teaching of Hebrews? Or do we reject it on this point? In answering this question we must pay due attention to the context of Hebrews' rigorism. The author lays down his principle not after apostasy has occurred, but before. What he is saying is that no one should bank on being taken back later if he apostatizes. He should face up to the serious consequences of his proposed line of conduct. The denial of a second repentance is analogous to the preaching of hell fire. In the NT it is used as an ultimate sanction before a contemplated line of behavior is adopted. It is not a situationless dogma with a general validity of its own.

The "Rest" that Remains for the People of God

Strictly speaking, the term "rest" in Hebrews is a soteriological concept rather than an ethical one. Nevertheless it has ethical implications, and we will therefore discuss it here. In the midrash on Psalm 95 (Heb. 3:7–4:11) the author elevates the concept to a central posiiton in his ethical exhortation to perseverance.

E. Käsemann made it the key to his interpretation of Hebrews. While acknowledging the typological framework, Käsemann sought the substance of the concept in Gnosticism. The rest, which corresponded to entering into the promised land, was the rest of the soul which had achieved the fruition of Gnosis. But the rest is for God's *people* (4:9).

At the other extreme, G. Buchanan has connected the idea of the rest with his notion of Christian Zionism. For him, the rest means peace and prosperity in the *earthly land of Canaan*, the same land God promised his people in the time of Joshua, a promise still unfulfilled. Christ's work has taken away the sins which prevent God's people from appropriating rest in the land of Canaan. If they hold on, they will eventually enjoy peace and prosperity in the holy land. This is a most improbable interpretation. The promise was in fact fulfilled when Israel entered the promised land and all her enemies were defeated. At the very latest, it was fulfilled when David consolidated the monarchy and gave peace and prosperity to the land. The "rest" of which the author speaks is not the same rest which was held out before the wilderness generation, but the typological fulfillment of their entry into the promised land, Canaan. Canaan is a type of the rest which is both future and transcendent. It is both because the author thinks simultaneously of two ages and two worlds (see below). Second, if Christ the high priest is our pioneer, the one who goes before us and enables us to enter where he is, then it follows that the rest will be the heavenly sanctuary where he is enthroned at the right hand of God. Third, if our author were addressing Christian Zionists who returned to Palestine, they would be already enjoying it, not still awaiting it.

With primitive Christianity in general, the author regards the Christ event as the fulfillment of the exodus. Hebrews has the same perspective on the heavenly rest as is implied in 1 Cor. 10:1–13 and John 6:25–59. All three writings seem to be drawing upon a common tradition in Hellenistic Jewish Christianity.

THE MILIEU OF THE AUTHOR

It has often been held that the author of Hebrews was a Platonist. Although the view has been seriously questioned, it still finds advocates, most recently M. M. Bourke. According to this view, Hebrews operated with a scheme of two worlds, an upper world of ideal realities and an earthly world where every empirical entity was a copy or shadow of its ideal counterpart. The Platonic interpretation can appeal to such passages as 9:24, which speaks of the earthly sanctuary as a "copy" of the "true," with its contrast of "shadow" and "reality." Usually this line of interpretation is coupled with a stress on the affinities between the author of Hebrews and Philo of Alexandria. This association is particularly plausible in view of Hebrews' other affinities with Philo, e.g., the use of Melchisedek.

Against this view we should note the following: Hebrews does not have a Platonic world-view in general. It is not concerned with the correspondence between all earthly entities and their ideal counterparts. Its language, insofar as it is Platonic, is confined to the correspondence between the earthly tent in the wilderness and the archetypal sanctuary in heaven. Moreover, this doctrine is not derived from Platonism, but is already suggested in the Pentateuch itself (Exod. 25:9) and was later developed in apocalyptic and rabbinic Judaism. Hence it is fair to conclude that Hebrews owes nothing to Platonism except the Greek terminology which it uses to describe this typological correspondence.

The dualism of Hebrews is a complex one. On the one hand it speaks about a correspondence between the earthly tent in the wilderness and the tabernacle of God's presence in heaven. On the other hand it operates with the dualism of two ages. This is indicated by 10:1, where Christ is called the high priest of the good things *which are to come*. The priestly institutions of the OT are a shadow of these good things which are yet to come, not merely of good things up in heaven. If the author were a thorough-going Platonist, Christ would have been performing his high priestly office from eternity. It could hardly have been inaugurated by a once and for all event here on earth. This complex dualism of two worlds and two ages is found also in the Dead Sea scrolls, and in apocalyptic and rabbinic writers.

Another suggestion for the author's milieu, popular in the Bultmann school, is that Hebrews is influenced by Gnosticism (Käsemann, see above). On this view, the Christology of Hebrews is based on the Gnostic concept of the *Urmensch* or primeval man. A modified form of this view was proposed by G. Bornkamm, who deduced from 13:9 that the recipients of Hebrews were syncretists. But the author himself is opposed to these tendencies. His Christology is entirely explicable as a development within Christianity. Its combination of wisdom's preexistence with royal exaltation Christology, and its emphasis on the human history of Jesus, its understanding of salvation as redemption from sin rather than illumination of our heavenly origin, is quite different from Gnosticism.

The Dead Sea scrolls produced in the fifties a kind of Qumran fever. It was suggested that the recipients were Essene Christians (C. Spicq, J. Daniélou, D. Flusser, H. Kosmala, and Y. Yadin). We have already noted the importance of the Melchisedek scroll. Buchanan sought to refine these theories by his theory of Christian Zionism.

What are we to make of all this? A clearer distinction needs to be drawn between the original audience of the midrashic sermons, the recipients of the written document, and the author. If the original audience was attracted to Qumran ideas, were the final recipients too? And how far did the author go along with either party? Was he reproaching them for not being better Christians of a Qumran type, or was he trying to wean them away from Qumran ideas? Probably the most judicious conclusion would be that none of the three parties was directly influenced by Qumran. Each of them emerged from Hellenistic Jewish Christianity somewhere along lines of development which led from Jewish sectarianism to later Gnosticism. Philo seems to stand upon a parallel trajectory of similar origin.

THE LETTER OF JAMES

The "epistle" of James is scarcely an epistle but rather a collection of moral maxims. They are disparate in character and are unified by the pervasive hortatory tone which summons the reader to lofty behavior. The categories are familiar Jewish ones, along with certain emphases proper to the emerging Christian community. If it were not for the initial greeting (1:1) and occasional phrases of direct address (1:2–5, 16, 19; 2:1, 5, 14; 3:1; 4:11; 5:9, 12, 19), it might not have occurred to anyone to put James in the category of correspondence. Nonetheless, the heading "Epistle of James" provided by a compiler and its placement in early collections among the catholic epistles (i.e., general; not addressed to any particular church) set the tone for the subsequent tradition. The designation of Barnabas and 2 Clement as epistles, despite the total absence in them of any epistolary character, likewise testifies to the practice.

In fact, the proper literary *genre* of this NT writing is parenesis. The Greek word means advice or counsel. It stands for a type of rhetoric closely allied to *protreptikos*, exhortation or encouragement. Parenesis often takes the form of a series of moral maxims loosely strung together. Parenetic literature further addresses itself to an audience either real or imagined, a fact which distinguishes it from the more impersonal sayings collection known as *gnōmologia*. There is nothing coherent or sequential about James even though there are groups of sayings within it and occasional returns to topics treated earlier. Common rhetorical devices such as concatenation (1:2–4, 14–15; 4:1–3) and diatribe (2:14–23) are frequent. Its central portion is 2:1–3:12 where three themes are developed: favoritism of the rich over the poor, faith and works, and sins of the tongue. Before and after this core there are shorter groupings of sayings, while scattered through the epistle are occasional aphorisms that stand alone. Two of these are: "The fruit of justice is sown in peace for those who cultivate peace" (3:18), and "Whoever knows the right course to follow and does not follow it sins" (4:17).

It is usual in treatments of James to pursue questions of authorship and audience first. Attention is turned fairly soon to the *crux theologica* that arose with the heightened appreciation of Paul in the Reformation period, the faith-works discussion of 2:14–26. But any such foreshortened treatment could miss the epistle's primary concern with various aspects of Christian behavior. Something different will be attempted here with an initial examination of the document verse by verse. If any clues are provided regarding the "James" to whom it is ascribed (1:1), they will be brought to light in this way. An excursus will follow on how faith (*pistis*) as profession and practice fits into the whole.

Presuppositions as to dating, provenance, and the like will be avoided in an effort to discover what conclusions, if any, assert themselves from the epistle. One preliminary remark needs to be made, however, namely, that the author possesses a good Greek style and only occasionally lapses into the translation-Greek of the Septuagint version of the Bible. Word-play and alliteration occur frequently and the opening phrase of address is quite elegant (only Acts 15:23 and 23:26 are comparable). James is written by a trained Hellenist who knows his Scriptures—a combination that says nothing about his being an ethnic Jew or non-Jew.

It is impossible to know at the outset from the writer's self-designation as "James" (1:1) whether this is his actual name or a literary ascription to some apostolic personage. The latter practice was common in the ancient world and has nothing of fraud or deception about it. Whatever the case, the earliest hearers or readers would have known from circumstances extrinsic to the letter the James who was intended. The use of the term, "slave of God, and of the Lord Jesus Christ" (1:1) may have been standard with Christians, underscoring their service of the God of Israel. It may also have had about it a self-conscious ring related to the use of the term by Paul (Rom. 1:1; Phil. 1:1; cf. Amos 3:7; Mal. 3:24 (LXX), and 2 Pet. 1:1). The address to the "twelve tribes in the dispersion" (1:1) is undoubtedly metaphorical for scattered Christians, all of whom considered themselves Israel without special reference to ethnic Jewishness. There do not exist sufficient indications in the rest of the document to force the conclusion that Christian Jews are the intended recipients. 1 Pet. 2:11, quoting Ps. 38:13 (LXX), addresses the readers as "strangers and exiles." The notion that "we have here no lasting city" occurs in Heb. 13:14 while 11:13, with its "strangers and wayfarers," harks back to the many biblical passages that describe the pilgrim status of the Jews. The "twelve tribes" is nowhere else used of Christians in the NT but does have a history in Christian literature of describing the whole Jewish people (e.g., Acts 26:7; 1 Clem. 55:6).

The proximity of *chairein* ("greeting," v. 1) and *charan* ("joy," v. 2) is an instance of the word-play referred to above. Vv. 2–4 immediately after the formal address resemble 1 Pet. 1:6 in their use of the Greek terms for "trials" and "testing your faith"; the "endurance" of vv. 3 and 4, a favorite term of Paul, occurs in the same context in 2 Pet. 1:6 as in James.

If a grouping of the early sayings is sought, it probably consists of vv. 2–15 with 16–18 as the conclusion. The theme discernible is the endurance of trial in faith which will lead to perfection (v. 4), or the crown of life (v. 12; cf. Rev. 2:10), or identification as the first fruits of God's creatures (v. 18). All three phrases are found elsewhere in the vocabulary of Christian salvation. Often the connection among the sayings of James is a tenuous verbal one like "lacking [in nothing]" (v. 4) and "lacks [wisdom]" (v. 5). This catchword technique is characteristic of the parenetic *genre*. At times it seems to be operative in this first section but at other times the links are so weak that we cannot be sure (e.g., the concluding phrases of vv. 8 and 11: "in all his ways"; "in all his pursuits"; clearer is: "Let endurance effect a perfect work [4a] that you may be perfect" [4b].).

The various indices of the generosity of God are paramount in this first collection of sayings. Unhesitatingly God gives wisdom to anyone who asks for it (v. 5); he is the author of every worthwhile gift and genuine benefit (v. 17); he wills to bring to birth with a word of truth (v. 18). The last phrase is redolent of a baptismal liturgy, although it could also refer to the working of the evangelizing process in the heart of a believer. In any case, it too has a salvationist ring.

The word of truth (v. 18) begets a faith that is proved (v. 3), a faith that is undoubting in which everything must be asked of God (v. 6). This *pistis* is clearly trust or confidence that the LORD will do as he has said he would in sustaining his people. It is the word which Paul invests with various meanings. Nothing in these early verses of James indicates that the word has Pauline connotations for him. "Your faith" (v. 3) is the state of mind in which the Christian cleaves to God. It is thoroughly trustful and is adhered to at a price, through test and trial. James accepts without examination the biblical axiom that afflictions sent by God can purify.

Opposed to faith is doubt (v. 6; cf. Isa. 57:20, the possible source of the wind-tossed waves of doubt and sin in this verse and 2 Pet. 2:17; Jude v. 13). Another enemy of perseverance in trial is the tug and lure of "passion" (*epithymia*, vv. 14, 15; in the Vulgate *concupiscentia*). This appears to be identical with the "evil impulse" of the rabbis, their favored explanation for the origin of wickedness in the human heart. It is the aggressive instinct or drive necessary for producing children, building a house, or succeeding in business. If channeled by obedience to the precepts of the Torah it need not be destructive. Otherwise, it leads to all the dire consequences spelled out in James 1:15. Desire or passion is strong in the human makeup. If yielded to it can lead to sin and actual, not figurative, death.

The sin of the doubter in James (1:8) is that he is of two minds (*dipsychos*; cf. 4:8), a word for instability which frequently occurs in 1 Clement and especially Hermas. The rich man's withering "like a flower of the field" (vv. 10 f.) is a special case of the fading of human glory (cf. Isa. 40:6 f.; Job 14:2). Why the rich man should be singled out by James is not clear. The "brother" in his lowliness (v. 9) is evidently the Christian who is being invited to exult in the paradox of his exaltation. The rich man's contrasted fate of being brought low is something he can hardly be expected to glory in! The irony is unmistakable. James' source is Jer. 9:23 f. where the wise, the strong, and the rich man are all told not to boast of their endowments but only of knowing the Lord. Paul employs this warning of the prophet Jeremiah in 1 Cor. 1:31 and 2 Cor. 10:17, and the verb "boast" frequently. James' unhappiness with the wealthy and those in commerce will surface again (2:1–7; 4:13; 5:1–5). Attention shall be paid to it at the proper time. Meanwhile, the rich-lowly antithesis of vv. 9–11 does not seem to flow from the contrast doubting–trusting (vv. 5–7) or lead to that of the enduring–yielding of the tested in vv. 12–15. The clusters of sayings are too disparate to suggest any such links. They are simply a selection from the rich storehouse of Jewish wisdom literature. God can raise up and God can bring low. He is the Holy One and he is not to be named as the source of evil, which is always a human affair (v. 13).

V. 12 is in the form of a beatitude, familiar from Ps. 1:1 and the sermon on the mount (Matt. 5:3–11). The usage will recur in 1:25c. V. 16 is likewise a well-known formula from the Greek diatribe, a contrived conversation and not a scolding as in modern usage. Its opening phrase, "Be not deceived," is found in Paul at 1 Cor. 6:9; 15:33 and Gal. 6:7. Here it is a reminder that God cannot be the author of anything bad such as temptation. The first part of v. 17 may be an unidentified snatch of poetry. The "lights" are stars and planets in the Bible. In the Damascus Document, God is "Prince of Lights" (chap. V). His unchanging quality contrasted with human changeableness is a convention of Greek philosophy, taken over by Philo.

The advice against hasty or angry speech in 1:19b reflects aphorisms in Prov. 14:17 and Sir. 5:13 and inevitably recalls the proverb, "Let not the sun go down on your wrath" (Eph. 4:26). But the cluster of sayings that v. 19 introduces deals with three things, not one: hearing, speaking, and growing angry (v. 19). Thus, the "implanted word" of 21b which "can save" is to be acted on (vv. 22–25). The meek or humble spirit in which it is received is not paramount (v. 21b); it comes only as an antithesis to the anger and filthy and vicious excesses which must be put away (vv. 20–21a). The Epistle of Barnabas knows about an "implanted" grace (1:2) and gift (9:9), a usage which helps identify the participial adjective of 21b as Christian rather than philosophical with the innate spiritual endowments of that discipline.

The mirror figure of vv. 23 f. has puzzled many in recent generations unacquainted with the imperfect metal mirrors of antiquity and their infrequent use by ordinary people. The two verses are self-contained. They are meant to illumine the sentiment of v. 22: put God's word into practice. With the introduction of the "perfect law of freedom" as the mirror in v. 25 the metaphor grows complex, in that the viewer *is* a hearer, not *like* one, but in any case a doer (v. 25b). As to the substitution of the phrase "perfect law" for "word," the gospel *about* Jesus Christ may be meant (cf. 2:1) but the whole tenor of the epistle suggests that the teaching *of* Jesus himself will suffice. At the same time, stress should not be laid on Christian teaching as the only reality that could be so described. The Jews of Jesus' day were convinced that the law was a perfect work because it was given by God and that adherence to it liberated. The phrase, therefore, could just as readily be pre-Christian as Christian. No antithesis to Mosaic law should be assigned to the words "perfect" and "freedom." In 25b James has the hearer as a "doer in deed." It was unthinkable for a Jew to be otherwise.

The person of uncontrolled tongue can scarcely be called devout (*thrēskos*, v. 26). "Vain" is the word for his religion (*thrēskeia*). "Pure religion" (v. 27) is defined in biblical terms of relief of the destitute (cf. Exod. 22:22) and a state of being unstained by the world. The second phrase is the more puzzling of the two. It recalls the "all that is filthy" of v. 21. Hermas' *Shepherd* has the same word as v. 27 for "unstained" (Vision IV, 3, 5) and in two other places it contains James' counsel on widows and orphans. Is the stain or blemish (cf. Eph. 5:27) related to chastity in James? The remainder of the phrase "by this world" argues for a general moral purity, not freedom from sexual lust in particular.

The fact that this Christian writer can speak of the "perfect law of liberty" in terms of good works when he comes to define what the law requires indicates that he is not much influenced by either rabbinic interpretations or Paul's view of faith as liberation from the works of the law. Writings such as Sirach and the Wisdom of Solomon and the moral maxims of Jesus are his guides in ethics and piety. There is no hint here of the tragic break with Judaism that was to distinguish Christianity in subsequent ages.

In chapter 2 there begins what was earlier designated in these pages as the central portion of the treatise: the admonitions against favoritism (2:1), against faith without works (v. 14), and against sins of speech (3:2). All three are prefaced by the address "my brothers." There is more coherence within each treatment than in the looser sayings-collections of chapter 1. The style of the diatribe with its rhetorical questions, numerous imperatives, and swift movement from one example to another marks all three sets of admonitions. If faith in "our glorious Lord Jesus Christ" is at odds with lack of patience or with doubt (1:3, 6), so much the more is it with partiality to the rich (2:1).

James 1:1 and 2:1 contain the only two references to Christ, a detail which made L. Massabieau (1895) and F. Spitta (1896) identify James as a Jewish document which had been Christianized overtly in these two places and faintly elsewhere. The opinion has not prevailed among students of the NT.

There is in chapter 2, overall, a tone of reproach or admonition such as might be found in preaching. This includes a direct charge of bad motives in 2:4 and sin in v. 9, with an invitation to speak and act in such a way that the "law of freedom" (v. 12) can be the judge. Faith without works is called useless or idle and the proponent of such a way of life an "emptyhead" (v. 20) in a bit of obloquy against opponents that was a commonplace of the period. Finally, there is the proposal that not many should become teachers since those who use the tongue much and sin but little are few (3:1 f.; cf. Matt. 23:10 for a similar injunction against the proliferation of teachers).

The discriminatory behavior of 2:2 f. is a made-up example to illustrate the anti-favoritism principle of v. 1, as is the casual heartlessness described in vv. 15 f. Hence, not too much realistic detail should be looked for in the two illustrations. James as a moralist hopes that his examples will have a deterrent effect but they cannot be taken as a faithful report of life in a particular Christian congregation, as distinct from Paul's correspondence. Viewing them as such would be to historicize a clearly non-historical *genre*. The author of James may have had experiences like the ones he describes but in employing them he generalizes. The musing of the unjust judge in Luke 18:4 is a similar instance to the fictionized conversations of James 2:3 and 16. In v. 3 the language is stylized speech such as might be used by an usher. The assembly (*synagōgē*, 2:2) is clearly a Christian one (cf. Ignatius, To Polycarp 4:2; Justin, Dialogue with Trypho 63, 5), which means that no case can be made by this usage for the Jewish origins of the document. The word *synagōgē* as a union or club continued in use apart from Jewish circumstances well into Christian times, just as *ekklēsia* was normal in Judaism for the ideal community. With the separation of Christians from Jews, *synagōgē* came to fall out of use as a Christian word. Little can be proved about the circumstances of the epistle by the term except that it is a first or second century document.

It has been much discussed whether this passage (2:5 f.) is one of the two in James that argues for a residual "piety of the poor" in earliest Christianity (cf. 5:1–6), meaning a self-designation of Christians as *ebionim* as contrasted with the reprobated rich. M. Dibelius is most closely connected with this view. It would seem, however, that the historicizing tendency he warns against in his commentary is better avoided altogether if James is to be seen as reflecting the rich-poor antithesis of common Jewish piety. Similarly, it is fruitless to argue the familiar or unfamiliar status of the rich man and the poor in a Christian assembly because both need to be shown to seats. That is scarcely the point; the point is rather the discriminatory, unjust judgment. A more interesting matter, as Roy Bowen Ward has pointed out, are certain rabbinic parallels with James 2:2 f. which suggest that a judicial assembly is being described here. The words "act as judges" and "bad decisions" (v. 4) would support this view. The same author holds that James in this passage is more interested in the well-being of the scattered Christians than in their personal piety, namely, that they should not engage in a debilitating factionalism.

James charges in 2:6, "You treat the poor badly." One senses that he has in mind widespread conduct. He moves from this to three charges against the rich, as if by reminding Christians of the classic opposition of the rich to the poor he has clinched his argument for the folly of making any alignments with them. There seems to be no relation between the "haling into courts" of v. 6c and the judiciary imagery of v. 4. The second mention is only a familiar type of harassment by the wealthy. The blasphemy against the "honorable name that has been invoked on you" (v. 7) probably does not connote calculated persecution, any more than the offenses of the rich of 6b and c do. We are led rather to assume ridicule of Christians which would include taunts about their religious affiliation. Here the closer modern parallel would be "Jesus-freaks" (cf. Ignatius, Ephesians 7, 1 and Hermas' Shepherd, Similitude 8, 10, 3).

The "royal Law" (v. 8) occurs as an adjective in Philo in his treatment of Num. 20:17, Yahweh being the king in question. The antithesis of James seems to be between favoritism (v. 9) and neighborly concern (v. 8b), behind which some are hiding in defense of their partiality. Otherwise the citation of Lev. 19:18b—with which James concurs wholeheartedly—would not make sense here. Favoritism makes one a "transgressor" (v. 9), and James agrees with the rabbinic principle that sees in the offender against one precept a failure in all (v. 10; cf. Gal. 5:3; b. Hor. 8b; *Midrash Bemidbar Rabbah* 9. 12). V. 11 spells out the solidarity of the commandments by recourse to the same divine authorship of two in particular, those against murder and adultery. He has caught his hypothetical favorers of the rich transgressing a commandment that has been singled out by the rabbis and Jesus, viz., love of fellow-countrymen as oneself. Hence he is sure that they have set the "royal law" aside in its entirety. An important theme in Matthew's Gospel is the threat of divine judgment on those who counsel departure from the law. This is echoed in the sanction proposed in v. 12 (cf. 1:25 for "law of freedom"), where "speaking" and "acting" are demanded. V. 13 is an independent saying about another matter, linked up with what precedes it only by the verb and noun for judgment. At the judgment God will not show mercy to the person who has not displayed mercy (cf. Sir. 29:1; Tob. 4:10 f. on almsgiving; Testament of Zebulon 5.3).

What follows next is a new train of thought except for a tenuous connection between "doing deeds of mercy" and "works." The notion that one can have faith, in the ordinary sense of "be a Christian," while not living rightly is challenged head-on. Such faith may exist—the author doubts it—but it cannot achieve salvation (v. 14). James then provides a comparison with the faith–situation rather than an illustration, by proposing a cheerful, thoughtless person who wishes another well while doing nothing to relieve that person's need. ("Go in peace," v. 16, is the ordinary Jewish word of departure and probably not a dismissal from the eucharistic assembly.) The gesture is useless in the circumstances. So faith "by itself" is barren, "dead" (v. 17).

In the imaginary conversation that follows, the author responds to the opponent's objection in 18b and 19. The fictional objection is itself obscure. We might have expected the reverse: "But [suppose] someone says, 'You have works and I have faith.'" The conclusion is unavoidable that the speaker is no actual opponent claiming to another that his or her works are superior to a faith without them. Rather, the author is hypothetically dividing the world into two camps, the doers (who presumably believe) and the believers without works. He then responds to the faith–without–works position of his division, not to the speaker of 18a ("You have faith . . ."), who from the outset was not the one to be reckoned with. In 18b James is ironical, intimating that faith without works in fact cannot be displayed, or if it is, will compare badly with the works that embody faith. He presses the irony to the point of absurdity in v. 19 by citing the demons who can recite the *Shema* (Deut. 6:4) but not without shuddering. This fearful reaction of theirs to God's name is featured in Jewish magical papyri. If James' opponents will accept as "faith" any enunciation of the statement that Yahweh is God and he alone, so be it. To the author it means much more, namely, a belief and trust in God shown forth in action. Some scholars minimize the actual existence of a faith–only position in any community of James' acquaintance, but he seems to argue his case too vigorously to be dealing with a hypothesis of no practical concern.

In support of his position that "faith without works is as dead as a· body without breath" (v. 26), James proceeds to "demonstrate" it (v. 20) for any opponent to "see" (v. 22) by having recourse to the examples of God's friend Abraham (v. 23 quoting Gen. 15:6) and the harlot Rahab (v. 25). Saint or sinner, a person is "rendered just" in God's sight "by works" (vv. 21, 25). The attack is on a faith–without–works position and contains no active defense of "my faith from works" (v. 18b) by the diatribe's fictional speaker. Interestingly, the phrase "by faith alone" occurs only in v. 24 in the NT, where it is denied as justifying. James has the well-known faith of Abraham assisting his works and these works then completed by his faith (v. 23). In addition to the justification of Abraham by his works (v. 21), the situation of Rahab is cited (v. 25).

It is impossible to maintain that faith is in the ascendant in this treatment by James, but for that matter neither are works. The author has no interest in a theory of preeminence, only in exposing the practical impossibility of the presence of one without the other. Quite simply, James presupposes that good works justify, as was the case in the offering of Isaac (v. 21). This is the Jewish assumption in possession. He does nothing to disturb it. But that the works of Abraham and Rahab were faith-inspired James also has no doubt. Their works were the manifestation of their faith, having first been enlivened or made efficacious by it. Faith and works together result in a person's being just.

A consideration of sins of the tongue follows which is a self-contained unit (3:1–12). Also this unit does not seem related to what has preceded. There is an opening admonition against seeking the church office of teacher which suggests that many were flocking to it. James discourages the trend by reminding them of the serious responsibilities incumbent on those who exercise the office (v. 1; cf. Matt. 23:10). V. 2a is ambiguous. Is it "we teachers" of v. 1 or "all of us"? The ambiguity may be intentional, for the sentence and indeed the whole verse serves as introductory to a diatribe on the tongue marked by numerous illustrations (vv. 3–5a). There follow an adverse judgment on the tongue (5b–8) and a series of metaphors on the contradictory purposes to which it is put (9–12).

The adjective "perfect" (2b) applied to one who does not sin in speech is the word used by Jesus in the sermon on the mount (Matt. 5:48) to sum up the "greater justice" (Matt. 5:20) of his disciples. James goes from this perfection to "the whole body" of a man (3:2) and a horse (v. 3). The notion of controlling the tongue has appeared in 1:26. The emphasis in the examples of the bit and the rudder, like the tongue (vv. 3, 4, 5), is on the large effect that follows from a small cause. Both are neutral until we come to the tongue, which is then illustrated by the negative image of the small fire which sets the huge forest ablaze (v. 5b). The tongue represents the entire "world of unrighteousness" (v. 6a). The imagery proceeds from defilement (v. 6b) to the taming of wild beasts (v. 7) to deadly poison (v. 8), with a stop along the way for being set afire by Gehenna, the dwelling place of Satan (the only NT use of this word outside the synoptic Gospels), and setting afire the "cycle of becoming" (*geneseōs*, v. 6c). The latter phrase is redolent of India's wheel of existence (*samsara*) but a more proximate source has come to light in the Qumran hymns. In 1 QH XII, 5–8 the cycle of night and day is spoken of, followed by the "births of time." The conception of human life as cyclic derives from the Orphic school of Greek

philosophy.   By the time of James the phrase he uses could have
become a commonplace for "life."

One saying worth remarking is, "The tongue no man can tame" (v.
8a).   There the exaggeration is rhetorical for it clashes with the
perfection envisioned in v. 2 and, in general, with the Jewish and
Christian assumption of the possibility of winning the mastery with
God's help.   The same rhetorical flourish occurs in the "we" who
bless and curse (vv. 9 f.; cf. Rom. 12:14), presumably Christians
generally and not just the teachers of v. 1.   Any such practice as
cursing is reprehensible in the Christian ethos (cf. v. 10b).   The
metaphor of James about fresh and brackish water is memorable.
That of fig tree and grapevine resembles Jesus' *logion* on figs from
thornbushes and grapes from brambles (Matt. 7:16=Luke 6:44).
Both are cognate with Stoic conceptions of harmony in nature, often
illustrated by the growth of grapes and figs.

With v. 12 comes the conclusion of the third of the three groups of
sayings that form the core of the epistle.   There follows (3:13–
4:12) a mixed bag of utterances against jealousy, envy, and strife
interspersed with warnings on covetousness, worldliness, adultery,
and slander.   There must be repentance and reliance on the God who
gives grace.   He alone is lawgiver and judge.   No one judges but
him.

The first cluster within the larger unit, vv. 13–17, is homogeneous
in the way it sets heavenly wisdom against all that divides.   The
qualities of this gift from God are spelled out (v. 17) after it has
been contrasted with an earthbound cunning that is animal, even
devilish (v. 15; cf. Sir. 19:22, 24).   The catalogue of evils recalls
similar lists in the parenetic sections of epistles such as Galatians
(5:20) or 2 Corinthians (12:20), while the praise of wisdom's qualities recalls Paul's ninefold "fruit of the spirit" (Gal. 5:22 f.).   The
only true wisdom for James, as for the non-speculative didactic poets
who wrote Job, Sirach, and Wisdom of Solomon, is derived directly
from God.

Perhaps the most interesting question in this section is the nature
of a wisdom that is *psychikē* (v. 15), falling between the earthly and
the demonic.   The term is part of Paul's anthropology in 1 Cor.
2:14, where it is rendered, as here, by *animalis* (Vulg.), "natural"

(NAB), and "unspiritual" (RSV). It describes the opposite of the man who perceives the things of the spirit of God. The wisdom James praises is from above (vv. 15, 17). The other type by contrast does not originate with the divine spirit. Were it not for the antithesis to *pneuma*, a spirit that is of God, one might be tempted to dismiss it as part of the Greek philosophical distinction among the terms body, soul (*psychē*), and spirit. But in the NT, spirit refers to God while anything "psychical" is opposed to him. In James as in Paul, this distinction is pre-Gnostic. The many who are "psychics," like the "somatics," are opposed to God, even as the "pneumatics"— few in number—are of his company. A fullscale Gnosticism is not being imputed to James here but only the working vocabulary of a growing religious trend.

The theme of 4:1–6 is that inner cravings yielded to (*hēdonai*, normally "pleasures," v. 1), allied with desire in its verb form (v. 2), are at the root of all dissension. Even when prayers of petition are uttered they are vitiated by a spirit that squanders what is received on foolish pleasures (v. 3). The charge, "You murder and are envious" (v. 2b), jars the ear. Its first verb is violently out of character with everything else in the sequence except, "You fight and struggle," in the same verse. The commonest way out of the difficulty is to soften "You murder" to something metaphorical about murderous intent, or else to say that overstatement marks the whole passage. A saying of Jesus, after all, equated hatred with murder (Matt. 5:22). The text tradition on "murder" is absolutely firm. This fact does not make the emendation "You are jealous", first proposed by Erasmus, any less attractive (cf. v. 5, "to jealousy"). A logical coupling would then emerge, "You are jealous and envious," leaving everything else in vv. 2–3 in the realm of covetousness and acquisition and the divisions they cause.

While this solves one problem it creates another of almost identical proportions. The original James may be saved from a gross inconsistency in speech but what is to be said of the early Christian copyist who first introduced the unlikely verb "murder"? The tendency in manuscript transmission is to soften phrases and solve problems, not to create them. The sole-attested reading, "You murder," at least does not create the problems caused by the calculated change of some Christian scribe.

Since the charge that some Christians are "adulteresses" (v. 4) follows the severe imputation of murder it does not seem so out of place. The meaning is almost certainly infidelity in the biblical, prophetic sense (cf. Hos. 1–3 on Israel as an adulteress and the people as adulterous; Isa. 57:3; Mark 8:38). The identity between friendship with the world and enmity to God indicates that stark oppositions mark this section. The covetous are murderous, they are adulterous, they are the sworn enemies of God. All this hyperbole may be interiorly consistent and include the notion of violence more readily than some commentators will allow. The author's problem is that of the compiler, namely, how to include the large number of disparate sayings available to him while preserving some appearance of an often nonexistent harmony.

V. 5 begins with "or" in Greek, an obvious attempt to link up what is claimed as a saying of "Scripture" with the opposition between God and "the world" of v. 4. The link has to be the jealous yearning (God's) or the tendency toward jealousy (humanity's) in this "Scripture" that no one has identified positively. (The quotation in v. 6 is obviously not meant by "Scripture" but rather that in v. 5. Other NT examples of quotations designated as biblical which cannot be found occur in 1 Cor. 2:9; Eph. 5:14; John 7:38.) Literally, the words of the maxim read, "Toward jealousy yearns the spirit that dwells in us." The first verb need not have "spirit" as its subject, however. The unexpressed "he," meaning God, may be intended, since the neuter "spirit" can be the object of the verb just as readily. Thus: "He yearns jealously over the spirit which he has made to dwell in us." RSV makes this choice, possibly following Dibelius; NEB and NAB continue in the tradition of AV and DRC (hence the Vulgate) respectively by making spirit the subject, as does *La Bible de Jérusalem*. Thus, BJ would read in English: "The spirit he has placed in us covets jealously. He gives besides a greater gift . . ." RSV has God yearning for the human spirit; jealousy is the biblical jealousy of God's concern to have Israel's exclusive worship. The BJ rendering is doubtless colored by a note appended to v. 5 which says that the same lost text seems to have inspired James 4:3, 5 and Rom. 8:26–27. V. 3 speaks of asking "badly" in prayer while Romans has the divine spirit interceding for us and helping us pray as we ought.

Clearly the translation of James 4:5 in BJ sees in it an echo of Rom. 8:26 where the spirit spoken of is divine and is at work in us. Since the divine jealousy is a loving one, the *de* of v. 6 must be translated "besides", not adversatively ("yet"; "but"). NEB and NAB go in an opposite direction by rendering this mysterious "Scripture": "The spirit which God implanted in man turns toward envious desires" and "tends toward jealousy," respectively. Both understand by "spirit" not only the human spirit but even the "bad impulse" of the rabbis. This would mean that this verse contains ideas like the oracle to Cain, "Sin's urge is toward you" (Gen. 4:7), or the word spoken to Noah after the flood, "The desires of man's heart are evil from the start" (Gen. 8:21). In such an interpretation, the "greater gift" or "grace" is that bestowed by God to help humanity overcome the envious tendency "which dwells in us." The quotation of v. 6 (cf. 1 Pet. 5:5; found in Prov. 3:34, [LXX]; its content roughly in Job 22:29) has God bestowing his favor (*charin*) on the lowly, an echo of the "greater *charin*" of v. 5 which will overcome the implanted spirit "turned toward envious desires."

The series of stern injunctions to submission to God and repentance in the next four verses (7–10) may have existed as a previous cluster, since putting v. 10 immediately after v. 6 with which it is cognate would have provided a better transition. The resemblance of v. 9 to Luke 6:21, 25b is inescapable, leading to the speculation that before the saying in James existed as an imperative it may have had currency in prophetic form. Similarly, the second person plural command of v. 10, which is not in the Bible in that form, comes closer to Job 22:29 than v. 6 does. The transposition of humble and exalted is a familiar *logion* of Jesus in the gospel tradition (Matt. 23:12; Luke 14:11; 18:14).

V. 11 continues in the imperative but goes in the new direction of prohibiting mutually detractive speech (cf. 3:1–12). It becomes in that verse a defense of the law and in v. 12, in the third person, a defense of God who gave it. Biblical and postbiblical prohibitions of slanderous speech are a commmonplace. Declaring one who judges a brother a judge of the law, not a doer or observant of it (v. 11; cf. 1:22), is something new. "Speaks ill of" or "judges" are two different offenses in v. 11. The notion of detraction leads to passing judgment as a means to reach the transcendent Lawgiver and Judge (v. 12).

Traders and the rich come in for further censure in the sayings grouped in 4:13–5:6, which begin with the aggressive "Come, now" at 4:13 and 5:1. The sin of the men of commerce turns out to be their pretentious planning without taking providence or the uncertainty of human life into account (cf. Prov. 27:1; Hos. 13:3; Ps. 37:20; Isa. 2:12). The fact that they hope to make a profit (4:13) manages to lump them in with the rich (5:1), in an imperfect parallelism. The boastfulness of the arrogant is repudiated in successive maxims (vv. 14, 15, 16), capped by one on acting in good faith that is totally independent (v. 17). Janus-like, it could look forward or backward.

Six verses follow containing reproaches addressed directly to the defrauding rich as searing as anything from the pens of the prophets (5:1–6). They recall Jesus' more measured speech on the same subject in parables like that of the rich fool (Luke 12:16–20) or the rich man and the beggar (Luke 16:19–31). The charges of hoarding wealth (vv. 2 f.), defrauding laborers (v. 4), and living luxuriously end with an accusation of the murder of the just (v. 6). This sustains the reading of 4:2 (the verb is the same), if both passages have under fire wealthy landowners with scant regard for human life.

A great variety of sacred and profane proverbial literature could be cited as background for these eleven verses. The pagan sources in particular underscore the brevity and futility of human life. But even though a phrase such as, "If the Lord will it" is a commonplace (cf. Plato, *Phaedrus* 80D; Minucius Felix *Octavius* 18.11), certain other language like the excoriations of boasting and wealth piled up unjustly is sufficiently proper to James that we assume he had real-life situations in mind. Moralists have certain bans that they hurl at the universe; the preacher's habit of castigating those far distant is well known. Still, there is every probability that James fears the actual incursion of the worldly mentality of business into the Christian community. The confessions of the wealthy Roman Hermas, suffering reverses as he wrote *The Shepherd* (toward the year 140), confirm this suspicion.

Certain phrases in James' fulminations against the rich are derivative (e.g., for "You fattened your hearts on a day of slaughter," v. 5, cf. 1 Enoch 94: 9; the acquisition of wealth by injustice, vv. 3 f., *ibid.* 97: 9 f.; the killing of the just man who does not resist, v. 6; Wis. 2:12–20; v. 18 appearing in the passion narrative at Matt. 27:43). The matrix of 5:1–6 is the general assumption of Jewish wisdom literature that the rich are unrighteous and the poor, by contrast, just. The eschatological tone of 1 Enoch (e.g., 98:3) is present in the reference to the last days, v. 3. For rust's devouring of flesh like fire (v. 3), cf. Judith 16:17 and Isa. 66:24—both of which feature worms as well. In 1 Enoch 100: 7 sinners are promised that they will be repaid in accord with their works, which include burning the righteous with fire (cf. James 5:3, 5). This is the familiar rhetoric of the pious poor who tell the rich to weep and wail over their sins. In James it fits into the End–expectation of the early Christians. Their religious speech was that of Jewish apocalyptic but we are unwise to speak of anything like "the expectation of the imminent End" lest we historicize myth and establish our uneasiness in its presence. The message of apocalyptic is one of sure vindication at an indefinite future time for clearly known cause. It has very little to do with sitting around waiting for the end of the world.

James ends with two collections of sayings, the first on patience and steadfastness (5:7–11), the second on varieties of prayer and penance (vv. 14–20). At that point the epistle ends abruptly. Sandwiched between the two final groupings and bearing no relation to either, even as they are unrelated to each other, is a warning against swearing by any oath and an admonition to speak truthfully (v. 12). (It closely resembles 2 Enoch 49:1.) Sir. 23:9–11 had forbidden swearing habitually by the Holy Name; the Essenes were opposed to oaths to establish the truth of what was said (Josephus, *Jewish War* II, 135); the strictures of Matthew's Jesus are well known (Matt. 5:34–37; 23:16–22). In 2 Cor. 1:18 ff., 23, Paul makes the case for unequivocal speech much in the manner of James 5:12. James requires a truthfulness so unfailing, whether one has affirmed or denied a given matter, that calling on God to witness the truth of what was said would be pointless.

V. 7 suggests patience "until the coming (*parousias*) of the Lord." The word *Kyrios* has meant Yahweh in 3:9 and 5:4 but here it almost certainly refers to Jesus Christ. The evidence from Greek-speaking Jewish sources on whether the term parousia was used to refer to God's final judgment is inconclusive; his "day" was the more common usage. In v. 7 the farmer is proposed simply as a model of patient waiting. Jesus' imagery in the parable of the seed growing by itself (Mark 4:26 ff.) has more to do with the absence of a human part in the dynamic of God's reign than with the patience of those who wait for it. Condemnation is threatened for those who carp against their fellows in the Christian community (v. 9a; cf. 4:11). The metaphor of the appearance of God (or is it Christ?) as judge recurs (v. 9b; cf. 4:12), calling to mind Rev. 3:3. There the one who was dead but now lives threatens a swift return like a thief—which is the present context; in Rev. 3:20 he knocks at the door seeking admission to dine. With the mention of ancient models of patience, the only name produced is that of Job (v. 11), unlike the lists of Sirach 44 ff. and Hebrews 11. Elijah will appear as a model for steadfastness in prayer, deriving from his perseverance with the priests of Baal in a context of faith (vv. 17 f.).

The ethics of the situation are explored in three cases in vv. 13–14. There is first proposed what to do if someone is "undergoing hardship." The answer is pray. If a person is in good spirits the prayer of song is fitting. If there is illness the prayer of the church's elders accompanied by anointing is indicated. In the latter case the double effect of restoration to health and remission of sins may be expected (v. 15; cf. Sir. 38:9 for prayer in illness). The anointing accompanying invocation of the name of the Lord recalls the exorcism of demons with the use of oil in Mark 6:13. The actual power resides in Jesus' name, the anointing procedure serving as an outward sign. The official "elders" of congregations, whatever their age, are evidently charged with a healing and forgiving function not given to all. This connection between power, physical and spiritual, and office is not paralleled exactly by anything in extant Jewish literature or the gospel tradition. The recipient of 1 Timothy is reminded of the gift he received as a result of prophecy when the presbyters laid their hands on him (4:14).

There is no reason to deny that the anointing of the sick with oil occurred in Jewish circles. We may assume from fragmentary evidence that it did. What is being affirmed is the emergence of a presbyterate with charismatic powers. The "prayer of faith" is what effects the restoration of the sick person to health and the forgiveness of sins if he have any (v. 15). Triggered by this possibility, the next verse proposes mutual prayer and confession of sins to all, "that you may be healed" (v. 16). That, "The vigorous prayer of the just person is powerful indeed" (*ibid.*), is given as the reason why petition and contrition are effective, as witness the case of Elijah (vv. 17 f.). There is no reason to panic at these verses and deny that they have any sacramental significance, or to maintain that they are the sacraments of anointing of the sick and reconciliation in the modern sense. James describes early Christian behavior. Sacramental rites have been developed since which look to these verses as their warrant.

The couplet with which the treatise closes tells the hearer to bring back the brother straying from the truth (v. 18), namely, from a just and upright way of life. The one who does so will save that person (v. 20) from death and will "cover a multitude of sins" by his own good deed (*ibid.*; cf. Prov. 10:12, the probable source but not in the wording adopted in James; 1 Pet. 4:8; 1 Clem. 49:5).

The data assembled in this brief review of the epistle show that James lies somewhere on a continuum that stretches from Proverbs, Sirach, Wisdom, 1 and 2 Enoch, Testament of the Twelve Patriarchs to 1 and 2 Peter, Jude, Didachē, 1 Clement, Hermas, and Pseudo-Barnabas. The cultural milieu is Hellenistic Judaism, the concerns are ethical with a religious motivation and purpose. Faith in Jesus Christ has not caused drastic changes in the view of righteous living of those committed to the biblical and post-biblical parenetic literature in Greek. It is largely fruitless to pursue the question of what is "Jewish" in the treatise as contrasted with Christian, as even the best of the older commentaries do. All is Jewish of a kind (not of the emerging rabbinic kind) and all is Christian. The two concepts are not antithetical religiously or culturally as they will shortly come to be.

There is no compelling reason from within the document to date it early, before A.D. 70, or late, toward 100. That is because we do not know what speech patterns did and did not characterize Hellenistic Judaism and the Christian community emerging from it well enough to assign a document to an early decade or a late, nor can we establish that the NT books it has most in common with (1 Peter, Matthew) serve as its source or derive from it. If the discussion of faith and works in James could be shown to be a response to Paul's teaching (as many hold) or to have elicited it (as a few maintain), arguments could be framed on the chronological distance necessary for the circulation of one set of ideas in the form in which they appear, to have been familiar to the other writer.

As it is, James' understanding of the problem he discusses is the ordinary Jewish one that good deeds are required in a believer. He polemicizes against anyone who might maintain that religious commitment has no practical consequences. There have always been such and, more commonly, there are detractors who will say that a given religious tradition makes no ethical demands. Paul's doctrine of saving faith goes in quite another direction. It leaves undisturbed the axiom of the necessity of living out faith by deeds. Paul polemicizes not against the doer of good works—whose presence in the community he assumes as normal—but the arrogant boaster who assigns saving power to them but none to God's deed in cross and resurrection. His teaching that faith is active in love makes this abundantly clear (Gal. 5:6, RSV and NEB). James does not deny what Paul affirms nor vice versa.

It is tantalizing to speculate on the debates that were in progress in Hellenistic Judaism on faith and works (viz., being Jewish and performing religious and ethical acts) when Paul and James joined the conversation from two different standpoints of belief in Christ. We have the researches of Büchler (1927) to tell us of *Sin and Atonement in the Rabbinic Literature of the First Century*. A. Marmorstein explores *The Doctrine of Merits in Old Rabbinical Literature* (1929). These volumes contain a quite complete record of the Hebrew and Aramaic-language traditions on the actions needed to atone for sin and the ways in which human acts were viewed as meritorious in God's sight. The emphasis of the rabbis was on the fulfillment of Torah in the accommodated interpretations of the oral law, as is well known. The emphasis of the Jewish sages in the canon (Qoheleth, Proverbs) and Deutero-canonical Sirach, Wisdom, Tobit, Judith and various extracanonical books (1 and 2 Enoch, Testament of the Twelve Patriarchs) was on living according to a divine wisdom which fulfilled the whole law.

Whereas much of the latter Jewish material is extant, there is no solid information on the relation of the Hellenistic Jews in Palestine and elsewhere to the reforming party of Johanan ben Zakkai (d. ca. 80) on trust in God and works of the law. We simply do not know the terms of the internal Jewish debate of the first century on this question, only of the rabbinic and Christian results as precipitated by Paul and by the separation of gentile Christianity from Judaism.

James provides one Christian view that accorded with one Jewish view. James is a Christian document but it is impossible to say how Jewish or un-Jewish it is because the record that would contribute to a solution is incomplete and those terms are wrong in any case. Anyone familiar with second-century Christian literature (the so-called apostolic fathers and apologists) will realize how strong and uninterrupted the tradition is of which James is a part. It is called—sometimes stigmatized—"Jewish" by those Christians who think that only Pauline thought on the subject of faith and works deserves to be called Christianity. James is not "Christian Jewish" in the technical sense of referring to the Jerusalem Christians of pre-70—about whom we have almost no information. James is "Jewish Christian" in that it reflects much that we know about Hellenist Judaism, with acceptance of Jesus as the Christ added.

As to the identity of "James," we are in the dark and fated to remain there. The argument is commonly made that none of the apostolic persons of that name in the NT could be sufficiently Hellenized in speech or at home in the Septuagint to qualify as the actual author. They include the son of Zebedee (Mark 1:19 and parallels), the son of Alpheus (Mark 3:18 par.), the brother of Jesus (Mark 6:3 par.; Gal. 1:19; usually identified with the leading Jerusalem figure of Acts 12:17; 15:13), the "younger" who is son of a Mary (Mark 15:40; 16:1), and the father of the apostle Judas, in distinction to Iscariot (Luke 6:16; Acts 1:13).

While some respectable scholars make the case for "the brother of the Lord" (d. 62) as the author, most interpreters consider James 1:1 a matter of literary attribution to this prestigious figure. It was that assumption which probably achieved the epistle's late acceptance into the canon (first cited as "Scripture" by Origen, then increasingly between Eusebius, 325, and the synod of Carthage, 397). It may seem cavalier to set aside the arguments that have been assembled as to which James, if any, was the actual author. The difficulty Paul experienced through Cephas with "those from James" (Gal. 2:12) has been coupled with the faith-works discussion of James 2 to identify the Lord's brother as the actual author, or as the person to whom this writing is attributed. A majority inclines to the latter view. The present writer is convinced that none of the companions of Jesus had a writing function but that the task fell to others of a later time in the various churches. The author of James probably chose the "brother of the Lord" as his patron because of his reputation as a just one (the description of Hegesippus quoted in Eusebius, *History of the Church* 2, 23; cf. Josephus, *Antiquities of the Jews* XX, 200, where the adjective does not appear). The compiler of these maxims was interested in facing judgment under the law (2:12), in how a person is justified (2:24), in the fruit of justice (*dikaiosynē* 3:18), in the fate of the innocent just person at the hands of his persecutors (5:6).

In aligning himself with Jesus' well-known family member, the author could also have hoped to capitalize on the very ambiguity of the James question. The perplexity of subsequent generations could have been the very effect he hoped to achieve by the wide net he cast. He is a "servant of the Lord Jesus Christ" but is designated neither as an "apostle" nor as a "brother" of the Lord (1:1).

The church possesses in James a priceless reminder of the lofty conduct that is mandatory for those who profess faith in Jesus Christ. Its standard and its social concern do not fall short of those of Israel's prophets but are easily their peer. Form-critical study of its maxims and of those attributed to Jesus reveals their derivation from common sources. Like Jesus, James is convinced that the law (the kingly law, the perfect law of freedom) must be kept. The one who keeps it does so because he or she is wise and possesses God's wisdom (1:5; 3:15, 17). Like the Jewish sapiential literature that it is, James sees observance of the law as an exercise of heavenly wisdom. In James, as in the religion of Israel, faith cooperates with works and is made perfect by works (2:22). Good deeds must be performed by the believer lest he or she fall victim to the divine judgment.

THE FIRST LETTER OF PETER

First Peter was highly esteemed by Martin Luther, who included it with the Fourth Gospel and the Epistle to the Romans as the foremost witnesses in the NT to the gospel which God had brought about through Christ. What attracted Luther to this letter was not only its closeness to Pauline thought, but also the triumphant conviction of faith which permeates it and challenges its readers to be in, but not of the world, and to endure unjust suffering in faith, hope, and love.

THE AIM OF THE AUTHOR

What did the writer himself intend to accomplish when he sent this letter in its present form to the churches of Asia Minor? In 5:12 he tells us that his purpose was to write "exhorting (consoling) you and testifying to you that this is the true grace of God; stand fast in it." His letter as a whole was meant to convey consolation, exhortation, and witness to Christians in duress, even in those parts of the letter in which the particular words, namely, consolation, exhortation, and witness do not explicitly occur.

Our author bears *witness to the grace* of God when he speaks of the election of Christians (1:1), of their call (1:15; 2:9, 21; 3:9; 5:10) of their sanctification by the Spirit (1:2), of their baptism (3:21), of their rebirth through Christ's resurrection (1:3), or through the life-giving gospel (1:23–25), of their membership in God's holy and elect people (2:4–10), and of the gift of grace which each one has received (4:10). The grace of God whose foreknowledge spans the ages (1:2, 20), whose prophets, by the Spirit of Christ (1:11), predicted the coming of the new age, has its focal point in the suffering of Christ and his subsequent glories (1:10–11). God's grace is manifested in "the sprinkling with the blood of Christ" which mediates and enacts a new covenant (1:2; Exod. 24:5–8; Heb.

50

12:24). Christ's death is God's gracious act of redemption (1:18). His blood is compared also with the blood of the Passover lamb of the End-time which has atoning power (1:19). His death is proclaimed as atoning sacrifice (2:24; 3:18), as vicarious representation (2:21), and as fulfillment of the role of the suffering Servant of God (2:22–24). It is also the power which liberates from sin and for righteousness (2:24b–25). It is the means which brings believers into God's presence (3:18), and it is the example for bearing innocent suffering (2:21; 3:17 f.). His resurrection is the basis of rebirth (1:3), the power effective in baptism, the reason why baptism saves (3:21), and why faith is simultaneously hope in God (1:21).

Moreover, the grace of God focused in Christ is synonymous with salvation yet to come at Christ's final revelation (1:13). At the same time, his grace is already present as power and loving gift which the author prays may abound in the present and which upholds the elect exiles of the diaspora (1:2). His gracious power "guards" them for the consummation yet to come (1:4). God who is the "faithful creator" (4:19), the redeemer (1:18), and the ultimate judge (1:17; 4:5, 17) "cares" for all who cast their anxieties on him (5:7) and "gives grace to the humble" (5:5). In the midst of suffering his "mighty hand" will strengthen them and ultimately "exalt" them (5:6–10). Until then, the elect and holy people of God live by God's grace in Christ through the Spirit (1:2, 12; 2:5; 4:14) proclaiming "the wonderful acts" (2:9) of "the God of all grace" (5:10), who called the believers "out of darkness into his marvelous light" (2:9).

The grace of God in its past, present, and future dimension, to which the writer bears witness, constitutes the basis and motivation of his *exhortations*. Upon these the emphasis of this letter lies. His exhortations for exiles challenge them to live "as obedient children," to be "holy" (1:13–17), to "put away all malice" (2:1), to "abstain from the passions of the flesh" (2:11), not to be "conformed to the passions" of their "former ignorance" (1:14), to "maintain good conduct" (2:12) as citizens, slaves, husbands (2:13–3:7) and to bear unjust suffering (2:18–25). With respect to their life within the Christian brotherhood, they are to "love one another earnestly" (1:22), "all of you be of the same mind, have sympathy, love of the brother, be compassionate and humble-minded" (3:8; cf. 4:8–10;

5:5). In their relationships to outsiders, the author of 1 Peter charges, "Do not return evil for evil or abuse for abuse, but on the contrary, bless, for to this you have been called" (3:8–9). Grace received is to be expressed in everyday life and its relationships, otherwise it becomes a pretext for doing evil (2:16). The many exhortations for exiles living in a more or less hostile world direct them to live individually and collectively by God's grace in its past, present, and future dimension. They are to be "holy" in the totality of their conduct because the God who is holy has made them to be holy "through the sanctification by the Spirit" (1:2), or, what is the same, through rebirth in baptism (1:3, 22 f.; 2:2; 3:21) and through incorporation into his "holy nation." By God's gracious election, they are a "holy body of priests." Individually and corporately, their purpose is to offer sacrifices prompted by the Spirit which are acceptable to God, through Christ (2:5). To deny that the "body of priests" is made up of priests is to deny that the elect and holy nation (2:9) is made up of elect and reborn members (1:2 f.) or that the brotherhood throughout the world (2:17; 5:9) is made up of brothers who are to practice brotherly love (1:22; 3:8; 4:8 f.). Christians are priests because they belong to the body of priests, even as they are living stones because they belong to God's house or temple (2:4). Their function as priests, namely, to offer spiritual sacrifice, is not further defined in 1 Peter, but it is fair to assume that it includes not only the exhortations "be holy in all your conduct" (1:15), proclaim God's wonderful acts by word and deed (2:9), but also access to God (3:18c) and the offering of prayer (3:7). Above all, it excludes mediation between God and the believer by a cadre of priests.

The admonition to express holiness of life is supported by the doctrine of judgment according to works (1:17; cf. 2 Cor. 5:10; Rom. 2:6–11; Gal. 6:7). This doctrine does not introduce a new work righteousness, but it does call attention to the problem of whether or not God's grace is misused as a pretext for evil. Election, redemption, rebirth in 1 Peter are also by grace alone. But even as in Jesus' parable the prodigal son who is accepted into God's house can and dare no longer live among the swine, so likewise the exiles of 1 Peter dare no longer do "what pagans like to do" (4:3; 1:14). The imperative "conduct yourselves with reverence" (*phobos*) toward God (1:17) points out that the goal of faith still lies ahead (1:9,

13). This reverence is not the terror of the judgment to come, but the reverence and awe before the judge who is our Father and Redeemer (1:17–19). Such reverence is the opposite of that arrogance which takes it for granted that God will forgive us because that is his business. Faith which does not find expression in "good conduct" is illusion and the final judgment will reveal it as such.

"Stand fast in" God's grace (5:12). This charge receives its urgency because the final judgment and the revelation of Christ's glory are believed to be imminent (1:5; 4:5, 7, 17). Signs of the End are the sufferings which the believers of 4:12 f. are already experiencing and which the persons addressed in 1:3–4:11 are likely to meet. Therefore, the author's witness and exhortations are also meant to bring *consolation* to his readers in the time of trial immediately before the End. Our author consoles his readers not only by recalling God's gracious acts, but by connecting their sufferings with Christ's sufferings and victory and by setting forth the eschatological glory in which they will share (4:13). He sought to give consolation by presenting their ordeal from a variety of perspectives which will be analysed later, and he made it clear to his readers that their sufferings were not indications that God had rejected them. On the contrary, the God who now begins his judgment with his own people (4:17) will himself see them through to the end (5:10).

Thus far we have inquired into the author's intention and found that his witness to God's grace is the foundation and motivation of his exhortations to exiles and of the consolation which he offers them in troubled times. While this indicates the author's purpose in sending the letter, we will raise three related issues. First, the problem of authorship; second, the problem of persecutions; third, the question of the unity of the letter.

THE IDENTITY OF THE AUTHOR, HIS PLACE, AND TIME

Our letter claims to have been written by "Peter, an apostle of Jesus Christ" (1:1), "a fellow elder and a witness of the sufferings of Christ as well as a partaker of the glory which is to be revealed" (5:1), "through Silvanus, a faithful brother as I regard him" (5:12), from "Babylon," with the church there and "my son Mark" also sending their greetings (5:13).

The fact that apparently no one in the early church questioned the apostolicity of 1 Peter favors the acceptance of the traditional view of Petrine authorship. Polycarp already quoted from it around A.D. 130, though he did not indicate his source. Papias also knew it, and modern scholars have pointed out that 1:8; 2:21–25, and 5:1 imply that the author of 1 Peter had been an eyewitness to the events of Jesus' life and death.

But the contrast between faith and sight (1:8) is common in early Christianity (e.g., 2 Cor. 5:7; Hebrews 11; John 20:29). Concerning 2:21 ff. and 5:1, we should remember that according to Mark, Peter was not even present at the crucifixion. Only Galilean "women were looking on from afar" (Mark 15:40) and according to the Gospel of John it was the Beloved Disciple and not Simon Peter who stood under the cross with Jesus' mother and "who saw it and bore witness" (John 19:26–37). Moreover, the word witness in 1 Pet. 5:1 signifies one who testified to the saving power of Christ's death, something the author had done in his letter. However, such testimony is independent from being an eyewitness to Jesus' death. Presumably many people saw what happened on Calvary without witnessing to the saving significance of that event.

Above all, the phrase "sufferings of *the* Christ" (5:1) reminds us of its prior occurrence in 4:13 where it refers to the messianic woes which usher in the End. Thus our author apparently made a twofold claim in 5:11. He also witnesses to the suffering of the Messiah by personally participating in the messianic woes. Therefore this verse probably alludes to Peter's martyrdom rather than to his being an eyewitness to Christ's crucifixion.

There are a variety of reasons for holding 1 Peter to be a pseudonymous writing. In its style and vocabulary, this letter contains some of the best Greek found in the NT. Our author turns some striking phrases (e.g., *aphthartos, amiantos, amarantos* in 1:4; our inheritance is "untouched by death, unstained by evil, unimpaired by time"; Beare, p. 57). He was also thoroughly familiar with the Greek OT (LXX) and could not only quote it, but chose words and phrases and combined ideas on the basis of the LXX. However, his expertise in handling the LXX is a literary skill, and does not reflect the knowledge of someone who had practiced the law himself before his conversion to Christ. The issue of the validity of the Torah, the heart of Judaism, has ceased to be an issue in 1 Peter.

The hypothesis that Silvanus (5:12) functioned not as a scribe who took down verbatim what Peter dictated, but as a secretary who composed the letter himself with instructions from Peter does not help either. Silvanus is not mentioned as the co–author in the prescript as he is in 1 and 2 Thessalonians. As a Palestinian (Acts 15:22, 40) he was no more likely to produce the style of 1 Peter and display the literary knowledge of the LXX than was Peter himself. Thus, the linguistic difficulty remains.

Moreover, 1:12 clearly implies that our author had not preached the gospel to his readers. But then we would expect that the historical Peter should give an explanation of why, in spite of the gentlemen's agreement of Gal. 2:9, he, the apostle to the Jews, would write a letter to gentile Christians including those of Paul's own mission territory of Asia and Galatia. Yet no such clarification is given in 1 Peter. If Peter had written this letter from Rome at the time when Paul himself was a prisoner there, then the failure even to mention the name of the apostle to the gentiles would truly be ununderstandable. When Clement, for example, wrote to the Corinthians (1 Clem. 47:1) or Ignatius to the Ephesians (Ign. Eph. 12:2) or Polycarp to the Philippians (Pol. Phil. 3:2; 9), they quite naturally referred to the man who had planted the gospel there. It is equally unlikely that Silvanus, acting as Peter's secretary, would have written a circular letter destined to be read also by Christians who had been converted by Paul, and who had known Silvanus as Paul's co-worker and yet not mention Paul's name once.

The main reason for assuming the pseudonymity of 1 Peter lies in its contents. It does not contain one single sentence which would indicate that its author had heard or seen the earthly Jesus. He did not even mention Jesus' words about discipleship, though he dealt with that topic in 2:21; nor did he allude to parables, miracles, or incidents in which Peter was involved (e.g., Matt. 16:16–23 par.; Mark 14:66–72). There are a number of parallels to sayings of Jesus. The most important are: 1:13/Luke 12:35; 2:12c/Matt. 5:16; 3:9/ Matt. 5:44; and Rom. 12:17; 3:14/ Matt. 5:10; 4:14/ Luke 6:22. 1 Peter knew some sayings which were incorporated into the First and Third Gospel. Nowhere are these parallels introduced directly or indirectly as sayings of Jesus, in contrast to Paul (e.g., 1 Cor. 7:10, 25). Nowhere are they treated like quotations from the OT which 1 Peter introduced with: "it stands in Scripture" or simply with "for" (1:24; 2:6; 3:10). The Petrine parallels to the sayings traditions are simply woven into his argument in the same way in which our author made use of common catechetical and liturgical traditions. Moreover, since in addition to quoting the OT our writer deliberately used OT words and phrases to advance his arguments, we can expect that he also worked individual phrases of the gospel tradition into his letter, e.g., 3:16/ Luke 6:28; 4:10 f./ Luke 12:42. (See Best, NTS 16, 1970, 95–113.) But a knowledge of segments of the sayings tradition and the use of verbal reminiscences does not imply direct acquaintance with Jesus himself, and the manner in which our author made use of his traditions excludes it.

None of these Petrine parallels to the gospel tradition is based upon the supposedly Petrine Gospel of Mark and none of the parallels is in a form more original than that found in Matthew or Luke. It was Papias who introduced the idea of a Petrine connection with Mark's Gospel (Eusebius HE III, 39, 15). Since Papias was familiar with 1 Pet. 5:13 (Eusebius HE III, 39, 17), the probability that he constructed the Petrine connection to Mark's Gospel on the basis of this text is rather high.

1 Peter also reveals the presence of Pauline thought. This does not imply a literary dependence on any of Paul's letters any more than the parallels to the gospel tradition imply a literary dependence on Matthew or Luke. The Pauline influence shows itself not only in the epistolary form of the prescript, but also in typically Pauline ideas and phrases, e.g., "in Christ" (3:16; 5:10, 14); "freedom" (2:16; found in the NT only in the Pauline and Petrine letters, and James); "charisma" (4:10); "sharing in Christ's suffering" (5:1; cf. Rom. 8:17); "not to be conformed to" (1:14 and Rom. 12:2); "grace" (5:12, etc.); "righteousness" (2:24). The connection between Christ's death and righteousness (2:24; 3:18) is typically Pauline, even though both passages in 1 Peter are part of a liturgical tradition. The offering of "spiritual sacrifices acceptable to God" (2:5) has its parallel in the "living sacrifice pleasing to God" (Rom. 12:1). The tradition of a social code for Christians (2:13–3:7; par. in Colossians, Ephesians, and the Pastorals) was apparently developed in Pauline communities after Paul's death.

While the influence of Pauline thought in 1 Peter is evident, we can also see that it is a late Paulinism which is reflected in this letter and expressed, for instance, in the terminology of "rebirth" (1:3; cf. Titus 3:5). One characteristic feature of the Paulinism which developed after the apostle's death is the absence of the discussion of the validity of the law of Moses for Jewish and gentile Christians. The burning issue of the Torah with which Peter and Paul had wrestled (Gal. 2:1–14) is no longer an issue in 1 Peter, even as it is not an issue in the deutero-Pauline letters. Also forgotten is the Apostolic Decree of Acts 15:20, 29, propagated by Peter and James, which demanded that gentile Christians "abstain from meat sacrificed to idols, from partaking of blood, from what is strangled (meat of animals not slaughtered according to Jewish ritual) and from fornication" (marriage of close relatives). There is no trace in 1 Peter of the Apostles' decree which placed certain cultic demands (Lev. 17:8–12; 18:6 ff.) on gentile Christians, even though 1 Peter is addressed to gentile Christians. It should perhaps be pointed out that in the light of Gal. 2:6, 10–14 and the discussion of clean and unclean food (1 Corinthians 8; Romans 14) Paul either did not know or did not accept this decree (contrary to Acts 15:22; 16:4). Since the authority of Peter and James stood behind the Apostolic Decree, its total absence in 1 Peter negates Petrine authorship. Furthermore, the Levitical, cultic purity demanded by this decree has given way in 1 Peter to demands for moral holiness also based on Leviticus (1:16; Lev. 19:2). The "abstaining" from certain kinds of cultic impurity (Acts 15:29) has become moral abstaining "from fleshly desires" (1 Pet. 2:11). In short, the problem of the validity of the Torah, which for a Jew always also includes the cult, is no longer relevant in 1 Peter. The reinterpretation of the Torah in terms of the demands for moral holiness places 1 Peter into a post-Petrine and post-Pauline period.

There are a number of other arguments which support the case for pseudonymity. First, to the best of our knowledge the Pauline communities were without presbyters, yet 5:1 f. presupposes a presbyterial church order which was introduced into Pauline communities at the time of the Pastoral Epistles and Luke–Acts, that is, toward the end of the first century. Second, the letter claims to have been written from "Babylon." Since we have no tradition which connects Peter with Babylon in Mesopotamia or with Babylon in Egypt, it is

commonly accepted that 5:13 refers to Rome. In what sense did our
writer call Rome "Babylon"? Moule suggested that Babylon sym-
bolizes the "place of the exiles." Such an interpretation is improbable because the letter is addressed to the exiles (1:1; 2:11) who
would then likewise be living in "Babylon" in which case 5:13 makes
no sense. However, Babylon is used as a cryptogram representing
Rome as the persecutor of the people of God (2 Baruch 11:1 f.;
67:7 f.; 2 Esdras 3:1 f., 28; Sibyline Oracles 5:143; Rev. 14:8;
16:19, etc.). This usage arose, however, as Hunzinger has shown,
after Rome, like Babylon of old, had destroyed Jerusalem's temple in
A.D. 70, that is, after Peter's death. If this is correct, then the usage
of the word Babylon alone would be sufficient evidence for establish-
ing the pseudonymity of 1 Peter. Third, the question might also be
raised whether the historical Peter would have simply called himself
"Peter" (1:1). This designation "rock," which was given to Simon,
son of Jonah, by Jesus, was originally a title of honor, not a proper
name. While others used it as a proper name (even as "Christ"
became part of Jesus' own name) it is rather doubtful that Peter
himself did so.

These and other difficulties suggest that 1 Peter is a pseudonymous
writing. Then, however, the question arises, what was the purpose of
this pseudonymous dress? Why should someone write under the
assumed name of Peter? Our letter intends to bring exhortation,
consolation, and witness to the grace of God to churches which suffer
persecution. The meaning of pseudonymity in this case apparently is
that "Peter" flanked by two "co-workers" of Paul and purporting to
write from Babylon/Rome expresses his solidarity in suffering with
the churches of Asia Minor (5:8–9). The pseudonymity evidently
serves the interest of consolation and exhortation. It is consolation
to know that the church of Rome and its great apostle Peter share in
the same sufferings which originated with the devil through the poli-
cies of Rome/Babylon. Our pseudonymous author presumably hoped
that his writing could gain acceptance as Peter's witness. If the fact
of Peter's martyrdom had already become known in Asia Minor, then
a letter bearing his name and being circulated at the time of a new
persecution might be even more persuasive because Peter the witness
(*martys* in Greek) to the sufferings of the Christ (5:1) had himself
suffered "as a Christian" (4:16), and glorified God by becoming a

martyr. The common kerygma (1 Cor. 15:3–5) which had united
Paul and Peter during their lifetimes ("thus *we* preach," 1 Cor.
15:10) was presented in a new form in this letter to churches within
and alongside Paul's mission. 1 Peter precisely in its pseudonymous
garb is a witness to the true catholicity of the church. The desire to
express the church's catholicity in suffering and witness, in exhortation and consolation, rather than the desire of the Roman church to
extend its influence into Asia Minor (so W. Bauer) would seem to lie
behind the pseudonymity of our letter.

That 1 Peter had actually been sent from Rome as it claims to
have been is, indeed, a possibility, but at least equally possible, if not
more so, is the hypothesis that its origin lay in one of the provinces
mentioned in the address (1:1). If so, the code name "Babylon" is
part of 1 Peter's pseudonymity. This cryptogram would indicate a
place of origin in proximity to that of the Book of Revelation, such as
Ephesus, which would also account for the presence of Pauline language. Incidentally, the code name "Babylon" does not appear in 1
Clement which was written from Rome.

It is notoriously difficult to establish a date for this letter. As a
pseudonymous writing it originated after A.D. 70. Since 2 Peter
knew of it (3:1) and Polycarp quoted from it around A.D. 130, we
are left with the period between A.D. 80 and 111 as the time of
origin.

PERSECUTIONS

Though the NT contains many general references to persecutions
of Christians, we owe our knowledge of Nero's savage persecution of
Roman Christians in A.D. 64, when Peter probably also lost his life,
not to the NT, but to Tacitus (Annales 15:38–44). Likewise, were
it not for the accidental publication of Pliny's letters, we would not
know anything about the executions of Christians which he instigated
in A.D. 111 in Bithynia, one of the provinces mentioned in 1 Pet. 1:1
(Epistles X, 96, 97). With the exception of the Apocalypse and, as
we shall see, 1 Peter, early Christian writers, including Clement and
Ignatius, did not dwell on the subject of the imperial authorities as
persecutors of Christians, but deliberately played down the government's role as persecutor. Yet from Pliny's letter and Trajan's reply,
we must conclude that the execution of Christians who refused to

apostatize and curse Christ was not the result of the introduction of a
new criminal law in A.D. 111. Rather, Pliny followed procedures
established by custom, though he was uncertain about some details of
that procedure.   Therefore, if 1 Peter was not written at the time
when Pliny was executing Christians of Bithynia, because they were
Christians, then our letter was written at the time of a prior persecution about which we have no information except indirectly in Revelation 13 and 17.

In 1 Peter we recognize that the suffering spoken of in 1:6; 2:12,
19; 3:13–17; 4:4 is caused by defamation, vilification, and unjust
treatment.   Occasionally such "suffering" may have involved legal
proceedings (3:15), but a persecution initiated by the state is not
reflected in 1:3–4:11.   If we look carefully at these texts we can
also discover that none of them states that the people addressed have
actually undergone suffering already.   This is also the case in 1:6
which is one of several difficult verses in this letter.   For reasons of
space, we shall first paraphrase it and note a few grammatical details.
"When you receive your inheritance (1:4) and the salvation which
is ready to be revealed (1:5) then you shall exult even though now,
since it is the will of God, you will be distressed for a little while by
various trials."

Some comments: the verb *agalliaomai* in 1:6 refers to the future
eschatological joy in spite of the present tense of the Greek verb.   (The
present tense of the verb "exult" in 1:6 expresses the confident assertion regarding the "future" which is imminent; cf. Blass-Debrunner
§ 323.)   Its future meaning is also found in 1:8 which speaks of
"exulting with joy inexpressible and glorified," likewise using the
present tense.   However, "glorified (perfect passive participle) joy"
(1:8) can be ours only when the future salvation (1:4) and glory
(1:7) are revealed. Furthermore, 1 Pet. 4:13 clearly distinguishes between the *present joy* in suffering and the future joy.   The Greek verb
agalliaomai is reserved for the latter in this verse.   Thus we interpret
1:6: "In the imminent future when you obtain your inheritance and
your salvation (1:4–5), you will exult."   Hence, the subsequent aorist
participle *lypēthenthes* in 1:6 does not refer to the past sufferings which
the people addressed have already endured, but to experiences which
they will have to face before they obtain their final salvation.—The RSV
translation and quite a few interpreters propose that the Greek phrase
ei deon suggests that the distress of 1:6 is contingent and presented as

a possibility only. More probable is the interpretation that the distress of 1:6 is a divine necessity, *ei deon* having the force of "since it is God's will."

In 3:13, 17 we meet two Greek optatives which are usually interpreted as expressing the possibility, the contingency, of suffering. It is obvious that both optatives imply that the people addressed have not yet suffered as Christians. The question of whether suffering is merely a possibility, or rather a probability and necessity, requires that we take the context seriously. It would appear that our author up to 4:11 tells his audience that defamation and calumnies are the realities which they have to face.

We may summarize our discussion thus far: 1) There is nothing in 1 Pet. 1:1–4:11 which speaks of a persecution initiated by the state; 2) Suffering in this section is presented as divine necessity, or a likely possibility caused primarily by the defamations of the populace; 3) Such suffering may occasionally include legal proceedings; 4) Nowhere is it stated that the people addressed have actually suffered already.

The situation appears to be different in 4:12–5:11, even though most recent interpreters deny that persecution by the state serves as a background to this section. They point out that if the suffering were caused by the state, then 5:9 would presuppose a worldwide persecution of the church which obviously did not take place during the first or second centuries.

What is of primary importance for the interpretation of our letter is what the *author believed* was happening, not what actually took place. He believed that the End was already beginning in 4:17, though we today know otherwise. Likewise, he believed that the "fiery ordeal" of 4:12 would have a worldwide dimension even though we know that general persecutions by the state did not come until 150 years later. Furthermore, we should keep in mind not only the pseudonymity of this writing which forbade its author to be too specific about the situation, but also the hesitancy of NT writers to speak about persecutions by the state, even when they must have known about them.

It is also obvious that the "fiery ordeal" of 4:12 ff. was already in progress whereas up to 4:11 we hear of the necessity or probability of suffering. We will try to show later that 1:3–4:11 was originally an address to recently baptized converts. As members of God's people they too will face suffering (1:6; 3:14, 17). But in 4:13 they are sharing in it.

In the first section it is assumed that good conduct will generally be recognized though at times they will have to suffer (2:12, 15; 3:13–14). This assumption is absent in the second part and the rhetorical question of 3:13 would likewise be out of place after 4:11. The hope expressed in 2:14 that the government would "praise those who do what is good," a hope repeated in 3:15–16 where Christians, should they be accused before magistrates, can expect their vindication, has disappeared in the section beginning at 4:12. Christians are still exhorted to persevere in good deeds (4:19), but it is no longer expected that their good conduct will be recognized by the world.

In the second section the reproaches heaped on Christians no longer have their roots in the astonishment of gentiles that Christians refuse to share in their vices (4:3–4), but are now focused on "the name of Christ" (4:14, 16). Suffering no longer seems to consist primarily in verbal abuse but in the kind of punishment meted out to a "murderer, criminal, or mischief maker" (4:15). The juxtaposition of suffering "as a Christian" in 4:16 with a series of criminal activities in 4:15 seems to imply that legal action was taken against Christians in which confessing "the name of Christ" (4:14) and being "a Christian" (4:15) constituted the crime. (*Allotriepiskopos* of 4:15 is found nowhere else in Greek. Could it be an allusion to a crooked *episkopos*, bishop, who was justly punished for his misdeeds? Cf. *episkopountes* in 5:2, papyrus 72, codex A, and the phrase "not for shameful gain.")

We can also detect a shift in eschatology. In 1:5; 4:5, 7 the End is believed to be near whereas in 4:17 the *kairos* of God's judgment is already beginning.

To be sure, suffering in both sections is regarded as a test of faith (1:6 f.; 4:12), but only in the second part is it interpreted as the inbreaking of the messianic woes which usher in the End (the sufferings of *the* Christ, 4:13; 5:1). Only in the second part is suffering related to the devil, prowling like a lion (Pss. 22:13; 57:4; Jer. 4:7; 1QH 5:5 f.), and only here does Rome appear under the apocalyptic cryptogram of Babylon (5:13), the city which persecutes God's people (in distinction to 2:13–14).

In light of this we conclude that a regional persecution, probably in Bithynia and Pontus (mentioned first and last in 1:1, and thus highlighted even though they formed one Roman province) was the occasion when the letter in its present form was circulated. "Rejoice as (to the degree that) you share the sufferings of the Messiah" (4:13a). The forms of indignities may vary. Persecutions never brought martyrdom to all the believers of a region and pseudonymity hindered our author from being more specific.

In concluding this section we should recognize the developed attitude of our author toward governmental authority—an attitude superior to that of Rom. 13:1–7, though we should not forget that Paul did not advocate blind submission to governing authorities. When King Aretas, for instance, sought to imprison him, he did not submit but went AWOL (2 Cor. 11:32). For our author the God–given function of emperors and governors is to punish those who do wrong and praise those who do good. If so, then "submit" (2:13 ff.); but when that task is perverted, then "resist, firm in your faith" (5:9). Rome becomes "Babylon" as Christians are "reproached for the name of Christ" (4:14).

LITERARY UNITY

In addition to the differences noted above, we also find that allusions to baptism occur only in the first part (1:3, 15–16, 22–23; 2:1–2, 9–10, 24b–25; 3:21; 4:1). The interpretation of 2:2 is decisive for the argument first advanced by Perdelwitz in 1911 that 1:3–4:11 constitutes a homily to newly baptized Christians. "Like *newborn babes*, long for the pure spiritual milk that by it you may *grow up* to salvation; for you have tasted the kindness of the Lord" (2:2). First, we can see that in distinction to 1 Cor. 3:1 f. and Heb. 5:12, the "milk" is not contrasted in this verse with solid food. It is not spoken of disparagingly as something to be outgrown or left behind. This milk is called *adolon*, that is, without the deceit (*dolos*) which the reborn are to reject (2:1). Its second attribute is *logikon* which is usually translated as "spiritual." But this adjective also takes up the theme of the living, life-creating, and life-sustaining word (*logos*) of the gospel (1:23–25). The content of this "milk" is the "kindness of the Lord" Jesus Christ which the persons addressed "have tasted" already in their rebirth (2:3).

Second, the persons addressed are compared to *newborn babes*, literally to "recently begotten embryos." Frequently interpreters (Moule, etc.) have tried to show that in the light of Mark 9:42 this comparison applies to every Christian all the time. But this interpretation ignores the fact that our verse speaks of a process of *growth*, and therefore implies a process of maturing from their present state as recently born infants. The nourishment, the milk, will remain the same and can never be outgrown, but through it the persons addressed are to grow up until they reach the goal of faith, the salvation of their souls at the eschaton (1:9; 2:2b). The theme of spiritual growth stated in 2:2 is taken up in 2:5: "You are being built up as a spiritual house." This theme of growth also underlies the exhortations of 1 Peter. The combination of the phrase "newborn babes" with the theme of spiritual growth in 2:2 necessitates that we recognize the people addressed in 1:3–4:11 as newly baptized converts.

Also in Judaism a proselyte can be compared to a newborn child at the time of his conversion, not 20 to 50 years later. At his conversion he begins a new life in which he is to grow in obedience to the Torah (cf. Jebamoth 22a). The same is true of 1 Pet. 2:2. It would have been inappropriate to call people who had been converted some decades earlier "newborn babes." Nor did the author include himself among those newborn infants even though he is one of those whom God regenerated (1:3).

These "newborn babes" in need of growth will also have to face suffering as they join the people of God who are exiles in their own land. Hence 1:3–4:11 presents not a homily on baptism but a homily which gives exhortations for newly baptized exiles who live within a more or less hostile world. The modern preacher will do himself a service by reading this section in the light of his own sermons.

This hypothesis will do justice to the different situations and the different emphases found in the two parts of our letter. It also clarifies why this section is framed by a blessing of God at the beginning (1:3–12) which enumerates God's past, future, and present blessings and by a doxology at the end (4:11). The abundant use of the traditional catechetical and liturgical material in this section is likewise due to the original function of this section as an address to newly baptized members of the church.

Such a hypothesis also answers the problem of why the admonition to younger church members and elders is found in 5:1–5 and not in the section of 2:13–4:11. Neither group belonged to the newly baptized. It also explains why the theme of suffering is dealt with not in one section, but touched upon in 1:6; 2:12, 15, 19–23, then treated in 3:13–4:6, only to be treated once again and with greater urgency in 4:12–19 and 5:6–11. It also explains why the adverb "now" (1:6, 8; 2:10, 25; 3:21) is found in the first section only. At a time when our writer believed that the End was already beginning (4:17) in the persecutions experienced by the Christians in Asia Minor, he expanded his homily by adding 1:1–2 and 4:12–5:13. Through these additions the baptismal homily became a pseudonymous letter which, as a whole, aims at offering exhortation, consolation, and witnessing to the grace of God (5:12).

TRADITIONS AND THEIR USE

Our author was not a theological innovator, but a traditionalist. He did not advocate a "new" ethics of freedom, but articulated a theology of liberation, paradoxically through submission to God and to one another (5:5–7; 2:13; 1:23), and he exhorted his readers to a lifestyle of freedom which had its touchstone in the freedom to share in the sufferings of the Messiah (4:13). Above all, he used his considerable literary and theological abilities in the service of the tradition.

To clarify for his newly baptized converts what Christian ethics for exiles means in their context, he employed a rich variety of the traditions which were at his disposal. From the Christian exegetical tradition of interpreting the OT comes the combination of texts from Isa. 28:16, and Isa. 8:14 with Hos. 2:23 in 1 Pet. 2:6–10, a combination also found with the same textual changes in Rom. 9:33, 25. But our author expanded and reinterpreted this tradition by incorporating Ps. 118:22 (in 2:7) and by borrowing concepts from Isa. 43:20 f. (LXX), Exod. 19:6, and Exod. 23:22 (in 2:9). In addition to citing OT Scripture for the support of a thought, he employed individual words of OT texts or some brief phrases in order to develop a thought. Thus, for instance, while he cites 1:16 in order to support his exhortation in 1:15, he gives no indication that in 1:17–18 many of his words are taken from the OT and had already been used in Christian tradition.

As we have seen, the writer of 1 Peter also incorporated some sayings of Jesus from the synoptic tradition, as well as concepts and ideas that were developed by Paul and transmitted in Pauline communities. Furthermore, the sayings in which suffering is connected with joy (3:14; 4:13 f.) have enough parallels in other NT writings (e.g., Matt. 5:10; Luke 6:22; James 1:2, 12; 1 Thess. 1:6; Rom. 5:3; 8:18, etc.) that they can be considered as variations of an early Christian persecution tradition, which has its antecedents in Judaism (e.g., 2 Macc. 6:30; 4 Macc. 6:24–30; Bar. 52:6; Tobit 13:14). Among the parenetic traditions which admonish Christians to proper conduct we find catalogs of vices from which they should abstain (2:1; 4:3; cf. Gal. 5:19–21; Eph. 4:31; 5:3 f.) and catalogs of virtues which they should practice (3:8; cf. 4:7b f.; Eph. 4:2–3, etc.). The modern interpreter should not draw the conclusion that such vices were actually practiced by the churches addressed. As traditional material, they merely express what should under no circumstances take place among God's elect.

Space permits us to deal only with the christological traditions which in 1 Peter serve as basis for exhortations and to make a few comments on the social code.

Christological traditions

He was foreknown before the foundation of the world
He was made manifest at the end of the times. (1:20)

Its pre-Petrine form is recognizable by its participial style, by its pattern of eternal predestination–eschatological revelation and in the tension between the author's eschatology and the eschatology of these two lines. For the author the revelation of Christ is a future event (1:5, 7, 13; 4:13; 5:1, 4). In this tradition, however, the revelation is identical with the past appearance of Christ. His past appearance which was the result of God's eternal decree constitutes the revelation of God and signals the end of time. Our writer used this tradition to show that redemption with Christ's blood is anchored in God's eternal purpose which spans the ages and he added to this tradition: "for your sake who through him are *believing in God who raised him from the dead*" (1:21). The words in italics are probably a creedal formula which summarized the content of the faith (cf. Rom. 4:24; 10:9b; Col. 2:12c, etc.). Through his addition he told his audience that they themselves are the beneficiaries of God's past revelation in Christ; that faith comes "through" Jesus Christ—faith itself being the work of the revealer (cf. Phil. 1:27); that this faith is directed to God and his work of resurrection. Hence faith in God is inseparable from faith in the resurrected Christ and thus "faith is also hope in God" (1:21c, contrary to RSV). The liturgical tradition of 1:20 probably continued with 3:18d and ended with 3:22.

> He was put to death in the flesh,
> he was made alive in the spirit,
> he went into heaven,
> subjected to him were angels, authorities, and powers.
>
> (3:18d, 22; cf. 1 Tim. 3:16)

As in 1:20 so here each line begins with a passive participle and in 3:18d the two lines are also contrasted through a *men-de* construction. V. 19 did not belong to the tradition because of the position of the Greek participle and because the sentence is introduced by *en hō* which is a typical feature of our author's style (1:6; 2:12; 3:16, 19; 4:4). Also the sentence of v. 22 "he is at the right hand of God" did not belong to the tradition because of the present tense of its auxiliary verb and because of the sequence of the Greek text in which the going into heaven follows the sitting at the right hand. (The RSV changed the sequence into a logical order.) As in 1 Tim. 3:16 so here the antithesis flesh-spirit does not refer to Christ's human and divine nature, but to the two modes of existence. He was put to death as man among men, but God made him alive by giving him a divine, Spirit-permeated mode of existence. (Read 1 Cor. 15:44–50 as a commentary.) The climax of this hymn is found in Christ's ascension into heaven through which the conquest of all supernatural powers was accomplished. As in Ephesians (2:2; 4:8) so in this tradition the spiritual powers reside between earth and heaven. With this hymn, which was probably used at baptism (cf. 3:21), the Christian community boldly affirmed Christ's cosmic victory and hence his lordship over the world.   Those small, despised Christian groups knew and rejoiced in the world's true Lord ("And take they our life . . . goods . . . fame"; cf. Eph. 1:20–22; Col. 2:15; Phil. 2:9–11).

We now turn to our author's use of this hymn. He placed it in his subsection dealing with suffering (3:13–4:6) which the newly baptized will encounter.   This subsection had formed the climax of his original homily.   By announcing that the supernatural powers behind the pagan tormentors of God's people have already been defeated, this hymn provides the foundation for the beatitude of 3:14.   "If you suffer for righteousness' sake, you are blessed."   Such suffering is prelude to victory, to life "in the spirit" (4:6).   The antithesis "in the flesh" and "in the spirit" also provides the connection between Christ and the Christian in 3:18; 4:1, 6.   In order to orient his audience to Christ's suffering as an example, he introduced another creedal tradition adding to it the words "for" and "also" in 3:18a.

> Christ died for sins once for all
> the righteous for the unrighteous
> that he might bring us to God. (3:18a–c)

This creedal tradition combines the interpretation of Christ's death as atoning sacrifice for sins (cf. 1 Cor. 15:3; Gal. 1:4; Heb. 9:26, 28; 10:12; 2 Macc. 7:37 f.; 4 Macc. 6:28 f.; 9:24) with the interpretation of his death as vicarious representation.   Thus Christ's death is unique and much more than an example.   But an example it remains in that Christians who "suffer for doing right" (3:17) follow in Christ's footsteps.

His death is inseparable from his resurrection.   In vv. 19–21 our writer inserted his own commentary into the baptismal hymn of vv. 18d and 22.   His commentary connected Christ's victory over all demonic "spirits" with Christian baptism which was prefigured in Noah's salvation "through" water.

> The "spirits in prison" to whom Christ preached are not the spirits of dead people in Hades, but the fallen angels of Gen. 6:1–4.   In Jewish apocalyptic speculations these spirits caused the corruption of Noah's generation and all the subsequent corruption of mankind.   In Enoch 18:12–14 their "prison" is not below the earth, but at the "end of heaven and earth."   Their prison does not stop them from being active on

earth; it merely prevents them from approaching God. The spirits in v. 19 are identical with the demonic "angels, principalities and powers" of v. 22 even as the verb "he went" refers in both verses to Christ's ascension (Dalton).

The ascending Christ proclaimed his victory to these demonic spirits (v. 19) which means he subjected them to himself (v. 22). As God's judgment had fallen on Noah's generation, so it is now ready to consume the living and the dead (4:5). As God saved a few at Noah's time "by means of water," separating them from those who drowned in God's judgment so "now baptism saves" (3:21). It saves because in baptism Christ's resurrection and victory over demonic spirits is effective. It saves "not as a removal of dirt from the body but as a pledge made to God to maintain a good conscience" (or: "as a pledge proceeding from a good conscience"; or: "as a petition for a good conscience."). It would seem that the person to be baptized pledged that he would maintain a good conscience, that is, a right relationship to God.

Baptism does not save through this pledge, but "through Christ's resurrection" (3:21) which is effective in baptism, even as rebirth is brought about by God "through Christ's resurrection" (1:3). However, God's saving power effective through Christ's resurrection in baptism does not operate magically. It demands the obedient response made first in baptism and then continued "throughout the rest of the time of life in the flesh" (4:2). Negatively this pledge entailed abstaining "from the passions of the flesh which wage war against your (reborn) soul" (2:11; 1:14). Positively it meant to "be holy" (1:15–16), to belong to God's elect people (2:4–10)· and to exhibit conduct appropriate to it (2:12; 3:8; 4:7–10).

How is Christ's resurrection power effective in baptism? An answer is probably supplied by 4:1: "Since therefore Christ suffered in the flesh [i.e., died], arm yourselves with the same thought, (namely) that he who has suffered in the flesh [i.e., died] is finished with sin" (or: has ceased from sin).

Many interpreters understand 4:1 to mean that suffering if rightly borne purifies the flesh from sin (Selwyn). But a process of purification through suffering is excluded by the verb tenses in v. 1b. "The one who has suffered in the flesh (aorist, not present tense) is finished with sin" (perfect, not present tense). If martyrdom were envisioned in this section of the letter then "to suffer in the flesh" would mean to die a martyr's death which some Jewish traditions thought would atone for sin (e.g., 2 Macc. 7:37; 4 Macc. 6:28–29, etc.). But this is not the case, as we have seen, and as a glance at the peaceful community presupposed by the exhortations of 4:7–10 would indicate. Before proceeding further we should note several difficulties. Should *hoti* of 1b be translated with "because" or, what is more probable, with "that," introducing a sentence which tells us what "the same thought" is with which we should arm ourselves? Is *pepautai* in 1b perfect middle, "he has ceased," or, what is more probable, perfect passive, "he is finished with, he is removed from" (Dalton, p. 242)? Does the clause "Christ suffered in the flesh" (4:1) mean he died? In the light of 3:18, this conclusion would seem to be inescapable. But if neither martyrdom nor a process of suffering resulting in a process of ceasing from sin are acceptable interpretations of 1b, then we are left with the sacramental interpretation of the sentence: "The one who has suffered in the flesh is finished with (or has ceased from) sin." This seems to have been a traditional doctrinal formula which is also found in Rom. 6:7 with identical tense, voice and number, but with slight verbal variations. "He who has died is freed from sin." As in Romans 6, so here this doctrinal formula is connected with baptism.

To "suffer in the flesh" (4:1b) therefore refers to the Christian's death in baptism. Through his death in baptism he "has ceased from," or better "he is finished with" slavery under sin. In his pledge to maintain a good conscience (3:21) he had renounced his former involvement with sin. But this has to be translated every day anew so long as he still lives "in the flesh" (4:2). Therefore since Christ died in the flesh the baptized believer should have the same conviction which Christ also had, namely, that the consequence of death "in the flesh" is freedom from involvement with sin (4:1b). The conviction that by his death in baptism the believer is finished with (or has ceased from) sin should be the armor in which he faces the world. But all of this is true only because the Christ who suffered in the flesh (for our sins) is made alive in the Spirit and the believer's death in baptism is simultaneously his rebirth to new life. "Baptism saves . . . through Christ's resurrection" (3:21 f.) because the consequence of death in baptism is rebirth to a living hope (1:3).

We will comment briefly on 4:6 because it is another of 1 Peter's difficult verses and it concludes the subsection beginning at 3:13. There is every reason to hold that "the dead" of this verse refers to Christians to whom "he (Christ) was preached" while they were alive

(Selwyn, Dalton). Hence this verse does not refer to Christ's descent into hell preaching to the souls of dead people there. Christ was preached to those who subsequently died, that even though they died in the flesh they might live in the Spirit. This is the basic thrust of the sentence. Into it our author packed the contrast, "The way people look at it" and "the way God looks at it" (*kata anthrōpous*—plural; *kata theon*). How do pagans look at the death of Christians? Their death, like that of everyone else, is the common judgment "in the flesh." In that they are both right and wrong. Death is God's judgment "in the flesh." But that is not all. The death of believers is also entry into life "in the Spirit." That, however, can be perceived only from God's perspective or by revelation. The antithesis "flesh—Spirit" in 4:6 points back to 3:18. Christ was put to death in the flesh. Christians who die are judged in the flesh. Christ was made alive in the Spirit. Christians who die "live in the Spirit." Parallels to our verse are: 1 Thess. 5:9–10; Rom. 14:8; Wisd. 3:1–4.

The last christological tradition serves as basis for the exhortation of slaves and therefore facilitates the transition to our discussion of the social code.

Christ [died] for [us]
He committed no sin
No guile was found on his lips
He himself bore our sins in his body on the tree
That we might die to sin and live to righteousness (2:21a, 22, 24).

The author connected the tradition to the situation of slaves in v. 21b "leaving you an example that you should follow in his steps" and also in v. 25 "by his stripes you were healed," etc. Since the verbs of v. 23 are in the imperfect tense, not the aorist, we can safely assign this verse also to the author. Note the first person plural, "our sins"; "we might live" in v. 24 (lines 4 and 5 above). The tradition most likely contained the first person plural also in v. 21a (line 1) and the verb "died" instead of "suffered." The relative style of vv. 22 and 24 and the fact that their meaning transcends the context of admonition to slaves would seem to indicate that a christological hymn lies before us.

This hymn is unique in that it concentrates only on Christ's death combining the idea of atonement for sins with the notion of vicarious representation, and with the fulfillment of the role of the suffering

servant of Isaiah 53. Alluding to Isa. 53:9, it also affirms Christ's
sinlessness (cf. 2 Cor. 5:21). Even as the suffering servant of Isa.
53:4, 5, 12 took upon himself the sins of many, so Christ carried
them in his body on the cross, suffering the consequences of sins and
making atonement for them (cf. 2 Cor. 5:21; Gal. 3:13; 1 Pet. 1:18,
19). Moreover, the effect of the death of Christ is not only atonement for previously committed sins but also deliverance from the
power of sin to a life of righteousness (24b; cf. 4:1). This act of
liberation takes place in baptism. The original life setting of this
hymn is therefore most likely to be found in baptism. In his homily
to the newly baptized our writer used it as a basis for his exhortation
to slaves.

Social Code

Parallels to the social code of 1 Pet. 2:13–3:7 are found in Col.
3:18–4:1; Eph. 5:22–6:9; 1 Tim. 2:8–15; 5:4–16; Titus 2:1–
10; Rom. 13:1–7; in 1 Clement, Didache, and Polycarp's letter to
the Philippians. Antecedents can be detected in Jewish and Hellenistic popular ethics. Comparing the NT social codes we recognize that
their wording and sequence had not yet been fixed by oral tradition.
This means that a written catechism did not exist at that time. The
common elements of the social codes are 1) direct address, e.g.,
"slaves"; 2) the command, e.g., "be subject to"; 3) the motivation,
e.g., "on account of the Lord."

Even though the End is believed to be near (1:5; 4:5, 7) and the
persons addressed are exiles in the world, the social code directs them
to live within the social structures of the world and there to express
their obedience and love. The exiles may not make an exodus from
the world, nor cultivate a privatistic spirituality by withdrawing from
social obligations, nor contemplate the imminent coming of Christ
with apocalyptic enthusiasm. The social code of 1 Peter has a function similar to the social legislation of the Pentateuch. The people of
God who are separated from the world as God's possession must
simultaneously live in the world and for this 2:13–3:7 gives the
basic guidelines, with 2:11–12 serving as introduction and 3:8–12
as a concluding summary.

The imperative "submit" expresses the biblical presupposition that
authority comes from God, not from the majority opinion of the

people. It demands that obedience toward God and *agape*, unselfish love, are to be translated into action within social relationships. To put it differently, the Lordship of Christ which is inseparable from suffering and victory through suffering is to be made manifest not only in the worshiping community, but also in social relationships. Therefore, this imperative is broadened to the greatest possible extent. "Submit for the Lord's sake to every human creature." This sentence serves as the theme of 1 Peter's social code. (The RSV mistranslates the Greek word with "institution," but the Greek word means creature or creation. Furthermore, the imperative of 2:13 "submit to everyone" is parallel to the demand of 2:17 "honor all men.") However, submission to everyone in 1 Peter does not mean doing what everyone says. For instance, according to Plutarch, the submission of wives to their husbands included that wives must worship the gods of their husbands (Praec. Conj. 19). But such submission is set aside in all NT social codes. 1 Peter went one step further and not only challenged wives to win their unbelieving husbands through good conduct (3:1–2), but also called upon women not to be intimidated by their husbands (3:6). Blind submission is exactly what is not demanded here. In popular Greek ethics submission of the wife to her husband meant that the husband should dominate his wife. "Rule your wife" is a popular Greek maxim. NT social codes exclude domination of wives by Christian husbands. Eph. 5:25 exhorts them to *love* their wives, an exhortation unheard of in popular Greek social codes. Our letter demands of husbands that they be sensitive and tactful to their wives, to bestow honor on them, and to remember that both husband and wife are equally heirs of God's grace which consists in a new life. If a husband's new relationship to God does not find expression in his relationship to his wife, if his home becomes a hell-hole of dissent, then their prayers are "hindered", his faith becomes illusion (3:7). Such an approach was without parallel in contemporary popular ethics. Therefore the prayer found among Greeks and Jews alike: "Lord, I thank thee that thou hast not made me ... a woman" is absent in NT traditions.

We should also note that the demand for submission is related to freedom (2:16) and fearlessness (3:6; cf. 3:14). Freedom is the presupposition for submission and both are grounded in Christology and in reverence (of God; 2:18; 3:2). Therefore submission is rendered "on account of the Lord" (2:13), not under compulsion, but in freedom (2:16). For the Lord's sake Christians should submit to governmental officials and honor them as they submit to and honor every man (2:13, 17). Consequently, the quotation from Prov. 24:21, "Fear the Lord *and the king*" is changed into, "Fear God, honor the king." Christians do not fear their temporary masters precisely because they fear God. They are not servile menpleasers (cf. Col. 3:22) but they submit in that freedom which is modeled on Christ. Such freedom transcends both antinomian libertinism, the quest to express oneself in untrammeled fashion, as well as repressive legalistic pietism. The freedom to forego, to submit, is a lifestyle in which love interacts with the realities of the world. In his homily, the author still hoped that such a lifestyle would "put to silence the ignorance of the foolish" (2:15, 12).

Another feature of the NT social codes is the direct address, e.g., "slaves" (2:18). This too is a novelty, for slaves are not directly addressed in contemporary Hellenistic models. To be addressed means being recognized as a person. The NT bypassed the Aristotelian tradition, according to which a master could never do injustice to his slave, since as his property, his slave was not a person. It aligned itself with more enlightened views of the first century. To be sure, no one in the first century, not even manumitted slaves, advocated the abolition of slavery. Still, it would be superficial to argue that 1 Peter sanctioned the social status quo.

The rich man in his castle,
The poor man at his gate,
God made them high and lowly
And ordered their estate.

This approach to the social problem in terms of a hierarchical divine social order is exactly what is not found in 1 Peter. Nowhere in the NT is slavery or poverty regarded as an ordinance of God. However, 1 Peter gave new dignity to slaves by paralleling their fate of unjust suffering with that of their Lord and Redeemer (2:20–25). They, not their masters, are cited as models of Christian conduct when in freedom they bear unjust suffering and follow in Christ's footsteps. Thereby they exhibit the evil of an unjust society which tolerates and encourages unfair treatment. Christian conduct is not to be determined by the whims and ill will of pagans and slave masters, but by the Lord as model of the Christian lifestyle. This lifestyle includes the bearing of unjust suffering which exposes evil and seeks to overcome it by doing good. What 1 Peter calls for is not a passive attitude of infinite resignation, but an active demonstration of love (3:9; 2:12) which seeks to change evil-doing neighbors into brothers, because they are also God's creatures (2:13). The reciprocal love within the Christian brotherhood (1:22; 3:8; 4:7–9) is the goal of love toward the enemy in 1 Peter, but the latter is the criterion of whether or not the former is "unhypocritical" (1:22; 2:1).

In distinction to the social codes of Colossians and Ephesians 1 Peter does not contain admonitions to the masters of slaves. It would appear that the reasons for this omission lie either in the absence of slave masters among the newly baptized whom our author was addressing, or else he believed that slave masters cannot be true Christians. Here in 1 Peter Christian lifestyle shows itself in reciprocal submission and reciprocal love (1:22; 2:13; 3:8; 5:5) which is the opposite of the usual slave-master relationship. It is, however, improbable that the church membership of the regions mentioned in 1:1 did not contain any slave masters—see texts such as Eph. 6:9, Philemon, etc.

THE ELECT EXILES

The references to the pagan background of the people addressed clearly indicate that they are gentile, not Jewish, Christians (1:14, 18; 2:9 f.; 4:3 f.). It may seem surprising that gentile Christians should be referred to as "aliens and exiles" (2:11; 1:17) of the "dispersion" (1:1) when they are in fact living among their own kin and in their own land. Yet they are foreigners in their own lands because of 1) their election, 2) their worship of God, 3) their origin, 4) their lifestyle, 5) their innocent suffering.

Election signifies God's gracious design prior to man's obedient response. In contrast to Romans 9–11 the election of gentiles in 1 Peter meant that they inherited all the titles of honor which had formerly applied to Israel (2:9). All our author can say about the Jews is that they "rejected" Christ, the foundation stone of God's temple. They "stumble" over it because they disobey the word (present) "as they were destined to do" (2:7–8). The meaning of this difficult clause probably is that disobedience makes stumbling a foregone conclusion. If so, then no one is predestined to be disobedient, but if a person is disobedient then his destiny is that he will stumble. Yet one may question whether our writer made such neat distinctions. Perhaps all that 2:8 conveys is that God's purpose is carried out even through those who stumble, just as it is carried out even in the devil's hour (cf. 5:8 in relation to 4:17). At any rate, the line of demarcation between church and synagog is firmly drawn in 2:4–10.

The ultimate ground of the election of gentiles to be God's holy and elect people lies in God's foreknowledge (1:2) which spans the ages and designated Christ to be his elect foundation stone (2:4–6). It is possible that 1:1–2 incorporated a baptismal blessing which went like this: "chosen according to the foreknowledge of God the Father by means of the sanctification of the Spirit unto obedience and the sprinkling with the blood of Jesus Christ." Election is mediated through the sanctifying activity of the Spirit which operates through word and baptism (1:23; 3:21). The goal of election is indicated in a difficult phrase, "sprinkling with the blood of Jesus." Its background is not the blood of the passover lamb (1:19) but the blood of the covenant of Exod. 24:5–8, half of which Moses threw against the altar. The other half he threw upon the people who pledged, "We will be obedient." The election of gentiles should result in their obedience within the covenant ratified by Christ's blood and accepted by them at their baptism.

Once they were not God's "holy nation" but "conforming" to their pagan environment and "the futile ways inherited from ancestors" (1:14, 18; 4:3 f.). But now in God's great mercy they have been elected to be his people (2:10). Formerly they were "no people," aliens with respect to God (2:10) but at home in the world. Now they are "God's own people" (2:9) but exiles and aliens in their own land (2:11).

They are also aliens because they do not worship the gods of the land. The importance of this becomes obvious when we recall that polytheism and politics were inseparable in the Hellenistic Roman culture. By abstaining from idolatry, which functioned as the ideological foundation of the empire, the Christians were automatically an "out group" like the Jews. But in contrast to the Jews they had not received official privileges from Caesars. As aliens in an idolatrous world (4:3) Christians owe their ultimate allegiance to the one true God about whom 1 Peter cannot speak adequately until he has said Father (1:2, 3, 17), Spirit (1:2, 11 f.; 2:5; 3:18; 4:14), Christ (1:2, 3; 2:21, etc.). It is precisely "for the name of Christ" that legal proceedings were taken against them (4:14–15), and this in turn prompted the distribution of this letter.

Also their different origin indicates why the attributes alien and exile are indeed appropriate for them. They have been reborn (1:3, 23; 2:2), not "through corruptible seed" but "through the living word" and sacrament (1:23; 3:21). This means that faith cannot be understood exclusively in terms of existential decision. Baptism and faith are interpreted in terms of the miracle of rebirth. This concept is borrowed from Hellenism, but in distinction to the rebirth offered in Hellenistic mystery religions, 1 Peter does not think in terms of an ontological transformation resulting in the deification of the person initiated. For him rebirth is the miracle of a new beginning within a new relationship established by God resulting in a new obedience and lifestyle. This life is no longer under the domination of sin (4:1; 2:1, 24). The reborn shall also live by faith (1:8; 2:6), hope (1:21), and love (1:22), and they must fight within themselves the invisible struggle against "the desires of the flesh" (2:11) during the time of their sojourn "in the flesh" (4:2). Their regeneration stands under the same apocalyptic reservation (1:5, 7; 4:7; 5:6) which applies also to Christ's victory over the demonic spirits. (Even though 1 Peter announced their defeat in 3:19, 22 on the one hand, on the other hand the struggle continues and the devil must still be resisted, 5:8.)

God's people are foreigners in their own land at least partly also on account of their lifestyle (4:4). In a time like ours when antinomianism parades in our churches under the disguise of liberation, we would do well to listen to 1 Peter's exhortations, e.g., "Live as free men, but don't use your freedom as pretext for doing evil" (2:16). The people of God are not society on Sunday but distinguishable from society also by their lifestyle. It is not extraordinary feats that are expected of them, but the profession of faith and a faithful practice of that profession in word and deed. 1 Peter expected Christian conduct to have evangelistic power (2:12, 15; 3:1, 16). It is also significant that elders are to be "examples to their flock" in their conduct (5:3).

The position of God's holy and elect people as aliens and exiles in the world is accentuated by the unjust sufferings and defamations which they endure. In his homily, the author still hoped that through good conduct Christians might be able to avoid the taunts, jeers, and persecutions (2:12; 3:13, 16) but he also knew that in spite of that, they face suffering. He made use of several perspectives in interpreting innocent suffering to his newly baptized group. Such suffering constitutes "various trials" (plural!) in accordance with "God's will," which they must undergo "for a little while" so that the genuineness of their faith can be tested (1:6 f.; 3:17). This interpretation in terms of "testing" should be distinguished from the idea that suffering "purifies" the sufferer, an idea absent in 1 Peter. Unjust suffering leads to future eschatological "praise, glory, and honor" (1:7), and constitutes already now "grace before God" (2:20) which results in the beatitude of 3:14. Above all, innocent suffering is the manifestation of discipleship, of following in the footsteps of the suffering Christ (2:21 f.; 3:18).

Still the "fiery ordeal" struck Christians as "something strange" (4:12) and necessitated additional interpretations. Note that in the place of the "various trials" mentioned in the homily (1:6) which consist of chicanaries by pagans, we now meet the fiery ordeal and the final test (*pros peirasmon*, singular, 4:12). This final ordeal and test is interpreted by taking up the Jewish apocalyptic idea of the messianic woes. Before the End the powers of evil will make one final assault against God's elect. The nearer the End, the more terrible the ordeal, but the reverse is also true—the more terrible the suffering of the righteous, the nearer is the End (cf. Dan. 12:1; Assump. Moses 8:1; 4 Ezra 13:16–19, etc.; Mark 13:8; Rev. 4–21). Hence, 1 Peter interpreted the "fiery ordeal" which came upon the Christians of Asia Minor as being their participation in the messianic woes (4:13). As such, it is also the beginning of God's final judgment (4:17) and at the same time the manifestation of the devil prowling like a roaring lion.

But it is exactly the participation in the messianic woes that is cause for rejoicing because it guarantees participation in his glory

(4:13). Moreover, it becomes the occasion when the Spirit of God comes to rest upon the persecuted (4:14; cf. Luke 12:11–12), and when the power of "God's mighty hand" is experienced (5:5, 10), strengthening his people in the midst of persecution so that they endure "firm in the faith" until God "in his time" exalts them "to his eternal glory in Christ." Last but not least, the messianic woes embrace the "brotherhood throughout the world" (5:9). "One suffers as a Christian" (4:16) and is "reproached for the name of Christ" (4:14). In conclusion—the experience of various kinds of suffering also contributed to the self-understanding of the church as aliens and exiles in the world.

THE STRUCTURE OF 1 PETER

The letter has two clearly distinguishable parts—the homily of 1:3–4:11, followed by admonitions in the face of the messianic woes in 4:12–5:11. The whole is framed by an epistolary prescript (1:1–2) and by a concluding salutation (5:12–14). If we take into consideration that 2:11 with its address marks the beginning of a new section ending with the OT quotation of 3:10–12, and that 3:13–4:6 deals with the theme of suffering, we see that this homily, like many modern sermons has three parts, each having three subparts.

Epistolary prescript. 1:1–2.
1:3–4:11. The Homily: Salvation and obligation for the newly baptized.
Introduction. 1:3–12. A blessing of God for rebirth to hope, inheritance, and salvation brought about by the Father, through Christ, and revealed through the Spirit.
  I) 1:13–2:10. The Conduct of Christians on the basis of God's future, past, and present work.
    A) 1:13–21. Exhortation to obedience and holiness based on hope and redemption.
    B) 1:22–25. Exhortation to brotherly love through the living word.
    C) 2:1–10. Christ as cornerstone and the church as his elect and holy people.
  II) 2:11–3:12. Ethics for exiles within the structures of the world.
    A) 2:11–12. Introduction.
    B) 2:13–3:7. Social code regarding civil authorities, of slaves toward their masters, of husbands and of wives.

C) 3:8–12. Summary: Christian conduct in the church and in a hostile world.

III) 3:13–4:6. The conduct of Christians under suffering.

A) 3:13–17. Suffering in righteousness and fearlessness within a hostile world.

B) 3:18–22. Christ's death and victory, effective in baptism, as the basis of Christian suffering.

C) 4:1–6. Participation in Christ's suffering and victory.

Conclusion with doxology. 4:7–11.

4:12–5:11. Admonitions and consolations in the face of the fiery ordeal.

I) 4:12–19. Joy and confidence during the messianic woes.

II) 5:1–5. Exhortations to leaders and younger laymen.

III) 5:6–11. Final admonition and consolation.

Epistolary conclusion. 5:12–14.

FREDERICK W. DANKER

THE SECOND LETTER OF PETER

That the Second Epistle of Peter is a relatively late document (end of the first century to early second century) and certainly not from the pen of Peter, the Apostle, is almost universally recognized. More interesting is the question of the rhetorical unity of the document and its contemporary proclamatory value.

Of key significance is the opening paragraph (1:3–11), following the formal greeting (vv. 1–2). Its syntax has long perplexed copyists, challenged textual critics, and puzzled commentators. In the interests of smooth translation, contemporary versions such as RSV, NEB, the Jerusalem Bible, and Today's English Version obscure what is at first sight merely rugged syntax in the original, but in the process obliterate the contours of the fundamental solution: adaptation of the literary form known as civic decree, which would be very familiar to the readers of this very Hellenistic document.

A decree from the third century B.C., issued at Iasus, a city on the west coast of Caria in Asia Minor, displays the form in its most economic expression. After details of date it reads:

> Whereas Theocles, the son of Thersites, of Meliboea, has proved himself a perfect gentleman in his relations with Iasus and has rendered exceptional service to our citizens who visit Meliboea, be it *resolved* that Theocles, son of Thersites, be our public friend and representative; that he be granted exemption from whatever imposts our city has authority to exact, and that he be free to come and go both in war and in peace, without formality of treaty; and, finally, that he enjoy the privilege of a front seat at the games.

(No. 463 in Charles Michel, *Recueil D'Inscriptions Grecques*, Brussels, 1900. Details on the variations within the decreetal form and related diction in 2 Peter are discussed in an article published in the *Catholic Biblical Quarterly*, vol. 40 no. 1 Jan. 1978 pp. 64–82.)

Basic to the pattern is the interplay of Benefactor and Recipient, of the former's largesse and the latter's grateful response. Our writer's unique contribution, however, to the history of letters (supported by awareness of his formal departure from Jude's scheme) is his combination of the pattern Party B (Benefactor) acknowledged by Party R (Recipient) with a sequence in which the Recipient is urged to be a Benefactor, while at the same time anticipating a benefaction. The distribution of vv. 3–11 would then be as follows: Party B (vv. 3–4a) confers the benefit on Party R (v. 4b). Party R (vv. 5–7), recipient of the benefit described in v. 4b, acts as a Benefactor to his own community and reproduces characteristics of Hellenistic benefactors, as depicted in decreetal inscriptions. Party R continues to be viewed as a Party B in vv. 8a and 11, but now Party B of vv. 3–4a functions both in the spirit of a Hellenistic recipient of benefactions and as a benefactor (vv. 8b, 9b, 11).

In keeping with the decreetal pattern is the epistolary greeting (1:1–2), whose diction is not only Hellenistic (with *pistis*, ordinarily rendered faith, equaling "commitment to responsibility," and *dikaiosynē*, righteousness, equaling "fairness") but follows patterns found in decrees of epistolary form.

Awareness of the fundamental structure of 1:1–11 goes far to account for the writer's emphasis on the use of the tradition of the Transfiguration. Jesus, the Supreme Benefactor, has his credentials assured on the holy mount (vv. 17–18). Of chief interest, however, is the question of the relevance of 1:1–18, with its climactic affirmation of the Chief Benefactor's credentials, to our writer's preoccupation with the opposition described in the lurid tones of chapter 2.

AUTHORITY CRISIS

Pervading our document is alarm over a basic threat to the unity of the fellowship. This threat stems from an attempt to discount prophetic utterance in the past on the basis of disappointed experience, and to pit one apostolic word, such as Paul's on liberation, against another. 2 Peter therefore emphasizes the importance of the Transfiguration.

Not only is the Transfiguration proleptic and a guarantee of the apocalyptic windup, but the derivation of the affirmation (*carried* by the magnificent glory, v. 17) not only confirms its significance but is the prime factor in every authoritative word. This is the point of the conclusion expressed in v. 19: "And now the prophetic word is all the more established." That prophetic Scriptures are meant (and not necessarily excluding a pseudepigraphical writing such as the Book of Enoch, which was held in high esteem in some early Christian circles) is clear from v. 20. God himself at the Transfiguration confirmed that the prophetic Scriptures find fulfillment in his climactic action in connection with Jesus Christ as the Chief Benefactor of humanity. In practical terms for 2 Peter's community, this means that "the Day of the Lord" (cf. 3:10) will come, and its arrival is assured by the fact that its definitive character, "the power and presence of Jesus Christ" (1:16), had been observed in advance and confirmed by God himself.

To come up with a different interpretation, and specifically one that would deny the fulfillment of the promise of the parousia, and with it the termination of the world as it is now known (3:4), means to pit self-interested, or privately motivated interpretation, against the divine intention. But, as the writer emphatically states, it is a primary datum that no prophecy is to be subject to the vagaries of one's own hermeneutical decision (1:20). This conclusion is rooted in the fact that "no prophecy ever was *carried* through human initiative"; on the contrary, "human beings received their message from God and uttered it, being themselves *carried* by the Holy Spirit" (v. 21). Both the word *pherō* (carry) and the preposition *hupo* (by) in this last phrase echo the usage in v. 17. The affirmation heard by the apostles derived from "the most excellent glory," and the words of prophecy similarly derive from divine resources, the Holy Spirit. Thus, written prophetic word and God's action in connection with Jesus Christ form a unity to which the writer appeals in 3:2: "to be mindful of the words previously uttered by the holy prophets, and of your apostles' command, which is derived from the Lord and Savior." Since God's climactic revelation is Jesus Christ, the apostolic command itself rests in the majestic authority of Jesus as "Lord and Savior" (cf. 1:1), that is, Chief Benefactor. This authority finds confirmation in the divine voice (v. 17), which has consistently expressed itself in the prophetic word.

The divine word underlying the prophetic and apostolic word can speak with authority about the termination of all things, for the same divine word was responsible for the origin of heaven and earth "out of water" and for the destruction of the world through the instrumentality of water (3:5–6). Our writer parallels the fact of Creation and of the Flood with the fact of the world's present existence and its certain destruction. Between Creation and the Flood there was a considerable interval, and there is an interval between prophetic word about the End and the realization thereof.

In his peroration (3:14–18) the writer warns his readers against misinterpretation of Paul's writings. With the expression "wisdom was given to him" (v. 15), 2 Peter puts the apostle Paul in the class of the prophets who were "*carried* by the Holy Spirit" (1:21). The writer then goes on to strengthen this estimate of the Apostle's authority by classifying his writings with "the rest of the Scriptures" (3:16). At the same time he suggests that the "twisting" (v. 16) of Paul's writings is of the same order as the "private interpretation" denounced in 1:20.

Our writer's emphasis on authoritative guidance for the church is of a piece with his interest in the "godly" life, as expressed in his decreetal terminology (1:3, 7). Unified doctrinal formulation with a view to organizational consensus is therefore foreign to the thought that finds expression in this document, for this writer himself indulges in neologisms, even with respect to his authoritative source Jude. Nor is there any suggestion of an ecclesiastical teaching office as clearing house for correct interpretation. Rather, our writer is interested in the kind of instruction that maintains the proper relation between avowed allegiance to Jesus Christ and performance in the arena of everyday decision. Orthodoxy for this writer means to instruct the Christian community in such a way that present activity increasingly develops correspondence with expectation levels for the future (3:13–14). Out of such concern the writer's attack on false teachers develops.

In effect, 2 Peter's discussion of the prophetic word (1:19–21) constitutes a rhetorical bridge to the periodic bravura in chapter 2. Meeting the tacit objection that not all prophecy is necessarily of divine origin, the writer acknowledges that "there were false prophets among the people" (2:1). Thus the stage is set for the confrontation with the "false teachers" (v. 1). False teachers should constitute no more of a surprise to the community than did false prophets among God's people of old. In fact, as the future tenses in v. 1–12 indicate, they have been anticipated and are now current hazards (vv. 13 ff.). Contrasting with these "false teachers" are, of course, the "holy prophets" and "your apostles" (3:2). For this writer, then, orthodoxy means maintenance of purity in eschatological motif, in keeping with the apostolic instruction, to which he himself submits by adopting the pseudonym of Peter rather than introducing himself as fresh authority to the community.

CHRISTOLOGY, SOTERIOLOGY, AND ETHICAL RESPONSE

In view of our writer's emphasis on authoritative tradition it is evident that he could presume his reader's acquaintance with the principal contours of that tradition, including especially Paul's letters. From a methodological point of view one is therefore ill-advised to expect 2 Peter to spell out in detail what is already familiar to his readers. His aim is not to recall for them the details of their apostolic instruction, but to recall *them* to the importance of adhering to the instruction they already know (cf. 2:15, 21; 3:1–2). Much of Jack T. Sander's negative verdict on ethical content in the New Testament (*Ethics in the New Testament*, Philadelphia, Fortress Press, 1975, passim), and especially in 2 Peter, stems from lack of recognition of such presumptive approach by NT writers.

Examination of our writer's decreetal terminology lends precision to our understanding of his description of Jesus as "our God and Savior" (1:1). This is no metaphysical assertion, and it is not to be isolated from the writer's self-understanding. He stands in relation to Jesus Christ as subjects throughout the Roman empire stood in relation to their emperor and his viceroys. For them the emperor was *divus* (divine), and he could expect unreserved submission and loyalty. It is this dynamic aspect of anticipated obedience that 2 Peter aims to stress by his high Christology, and he underscores it by defining himself under the pseudonym of Simon Peter as a slave. "Slave" is the antonym of "master," and for the latter 2 Peter uses two Greek words: *kurios* (1:2 and passim) and *despotēs* (2:1). Jesus Christ is the ultimate authority over every human being, and he possesses it by virtue of his claim through purchase (2:1). Salvation, the supreme benefaction, has an indicative quality: purification from sins has already taken place (1:9), and escape from the defilements of the world is preterite reality (2:20).

Precisely in connection with this endorsement of Pauline "objective justification," more properly, "objective reconciliation," 2 Peter senses the point of origin of "gnostic" libertinism. Instead of recognizing that allegiance to Jesus Christ as Lord means the renunciation ("repentance," 3:9) of their former master, defined as "corruption" in 2:19–20, the false teachers construe the objective deed of Jesus Christ as invitation to self-indulgence. Thus, the "false teachers" and those who are capitivated by them live in contradiction to their avowed commitment (*pistis*, 1:1), which is to be intimately connected with the "fairness" (otherwise rendered "righteousness") of "our God and Savior Jesus Christ." Such is the twist Paul's theology suffers at their hands.

Nor is the slave of Jesus expected to function out of his own resources. 2 Peter shares with Paul the view that the Spirit is operative in the Christian, but this activity is described in terms of "his (Jesus') divine power, which has given us everything that pertains to life and piety" (1:3; cf. Rom. 8:3–4 and 29–30), as opposed to lust of the flesh (2 Pet. 2:18; cf. v. 10). Both terms, life and piety, are thematically and structurally significant. Life is opposed to impiety and lust, which are subject to corruption and destruction (1:4; 3:7; cf. 2:12, 19), that is, they have no future. Piety is the opposite of lust and unrighteousness (2:8–9) and the kind of life perpetrated at Sodom and Gomorrah (v. 5–6). To escape from "destructive lust" means to enjoy anticipation of a share in the Lord's divine nature (1:4), to be prepared for the judgment (v. 8) and to be equipped for the kingdom that is eternal (v. 11).

In his "climax" figure (1:5–7), 2 Peter conveys both the substance of Christian response to God's action in Jesus Christ and, by implication, its negatives. Faith (*pistis*, v. 5) is, as noted earlier in connection with the usage in v. 1, commitment, or acceptance of responsibility. The Hellenistic benefactor effects his commitment through actions that win the classification of "excellence" or "nobility" (*aretē*) in such discharge of commitment. Since the verdict of excellence is not won without unselfish expenditure, its opposite is self-interest and greed (*pleonexia*, 2:3, 14; cf. vv. 13, 15). Nobility in turn requires knowledge (*gnosis*, v. 5), for according to this writer, without knowledge one cannot avoid the path of self-indulgence. Hence he sets forth as primary his understanding that prophecy is not subject to the whims of the interpreter (1:20), and that in the last days scoffers will arise who live in accordance with their own interests (3:3). The false teachers, on the other hand, revel in connection with things of which they are ignorant (2:12). Since their ignorance is equated by this writer with self-indulgence (see esp. 2:10–14), and cited in connection with all manner of sensuality (vv. 7–22 passim), he emphasizes self-control (*egkrateia*), which has as its upshot faultlessness and blamelessness (3:14), in contrast to the blemishes of the false teachers (2:13). Self-control requires endurance (*hupomonē*, 1:6) in the face of a delayed parousia; the false teachers, on the other hand, selfishly capitalize on apparent nonfulfillment of the promise and bolster their position with an arrogant display of independence (2:10–12; cf. vv. 5–6). The antidote to self-indulgence is piety (*eusebeia*, 1:6; cf. v. 3), which expresses itself in awe before God's activity in history (3:11) and in submission to his lawful expectations (cf. 2:9). Such piety recognizes the value of community-concern (*philadelphia*, 1:7, our writer's substitute for the more usual *philanthrōpia*) and its concomitant, peace (cf. 1:2; 3:14); both of which are antithetical to "destructive party-strife" (2:1). Strengthening this sense of community is love (*agapē*, 1:7), which recognizes neither social nor intellectual conferment to the disadvantage or demotion of others; love is fundamentally respectful of personhood. The false teachers, however, with their ill-conceived sense of community, use their prestige to develop their own little fiefdoms (cf. 2:13–19) in opposition to the comprehensive reign of God (1:11), and direct emotions of affection into illicit channels (2:14, 18). Far from themselves having affection for people, they are, like Balaam, strictly in love with personal advantage (v. 15). By way of contrast, the true apostolic teacher does not seek his own advantage but the improvement of his fellow-Christians, his "loved ones" (3:1, 14, 17), even as the Lord himself is merciful to the sinner (v. 9). Paul, now deceased, remains "*our* beloved Paul" (v. 15). In related vein the Father speaks of the Son as his "loved one" (1:17).

In his concluding exhortation (see esp. 3:8–14) 2 Peter very closely associates his plea for moral stability with traditional cosmological diction. For the modern proclaimer and his audience, whose knowledge-bank includes information about planets in existence for millions and billions of years, and now even viewed at close range, such juxtaposition might seem to imperil the ethical imperative. In fact, however, our very increased knowledge of the universe suggests a fresh cosmological context for the conveyance of the writer's ethical earnestness.

Dominating his thought is a view of humanity under divine judgment. History has at intervals provided exhibits of this truth (2:1–8). One of the greatest catastrophes, the Flood, marked a change from one type of world to another (3:5–7), from the *kosmos* of that time to the present heavens and earth (v. 7). The very waters that were suspended in the heavens and confined in the earth (cf. Gen. 7:11) became the instruments (this is the point of the plural in the phrase *di'hōn*, "through which," 2 Pet. 2:6) of the earth's destruction. Man in rebellion is set forth against a universe that has seen radical changes in its structure. History itself gives the lie to the idea that the universe is stable. And contemporary probes of the heavens indicate that planets other than our own have experienced great changes, including life-support systems. The one possibility for stability lies in the ethical sphere, in commitment to benefaction of humanity through the power of the Supreme Benefactor. Along such a route (*hodos*, "way," is one of our writer's favorite terms) the individual finds his distinctive identity. Hence the writer contrasts the stability of Christians with the "errant" (the Greek word would suggest astronomical associations) behavior of the division makers (2:15, 18; 3:17).

Such stability in ethical decision, within the framework of the rubrics expressed in 1:5–7, is of a piece with the ultimate divine purpose, the triumph of righteousness (3:13). This triumph is independent of any cosmological metathesis defined in specific apocalyptic rhetoric, including that of our writer. God, however, will have the last word, and the Christian is committed to that newness, the ultimate realization of humanity, which spells the elimination of self-aggrandizing exploitation of one's fellow human beings, of the promotion of personality cults (which destroy the ethical identity of their adherents), and of the cynicism that extols individualism at the expense of the common good. To feel a sense of hospitality for any of these dehumanizing strategies is unthinkable. No rhetoric is too severe to express horror at their emergence, especially among Christians. Hence the writer borrows from Jude, along with much of his content, the form best suited for expression of such indignation: the diatribe.

DEPENDENCE ON JUDE

That 2 Peter borrows from Jude, not vice versa, is, like the pseudonymous authorship, generally recognized. The function of his variations from Jude's presentation is, however, of more than passing interest to the proclaimer of 2 Peter's points of view.

Jude's sequence is presented in two sets, each with three examples. Set A (vv. 5–9) displays examples of groups subject to judgment; set B (v. 11), examples of corrupt people, who are mentioned by name. In his adaptation of this material 2 Peter drops Jude's reference to "the people" who had been rescued out of Egypt (Jude v. 5), having mentioned a few verses earlier that there were "'false prophets among the people" (2 Pet. 2:1). This alteration gave him the opportunity to introduce the principal cause of the conduct that elicits God's judgment.

In keeping with the strong apocalyptic motif found in his source (Jude v. 6), 2 Peter begins with the angels who, according to Jude, sinned in the manner described in Gen. 6:1–4 and Enoch 6. Their example is crucial to 2 Peter's argument, being introduced with a monitory condition (2:4), whose apodosis is left to the imagination of the reader, who would correctly conclude, "If angels who transgress are not spared, how will mere human beings who engage in arrogant practices fare?" (see vv. 10–12).

Jude does not mention the generation living at the time of the Flood, but 2 Peter finds the exhibit important because of the contrast afforded between the rebels who were destroyed and Noah, a "proclaimer of righteousness" and therefore a model for 2 Peter's own generation of true teachers. Similarly he secures a confirmatory contrast between the residents of Sodom and Gomorrah and "righteous Lot," whose credentials are drawn not from the Book of Genesis but from a tradition that found expression in another part of the Bible,

Sir. 16:8. 2 Peter expatiates on his character in order to exemplify the virtue of *hupomonē*, a strong theme in his document and closely associated with righteousness (cf. 1:6).

In place of Jude's reference to a single angel, Michael, 2 Peter heightens the rhetorical effect by generalizing with the plural "angels" and underscores the arrogance of the false teachers with the description of these respectful angels as "greater in might and power" (2:11).

By eliminating the names of Cain and Korah from the triad in Jude v. 11, 2 Peter focuses the reader's attention on the moral deficiencies of Balaam, who becomes the whipping boy in the writer's expanded execration of false teachers (vv. 15–16).

Comparison of 2 Peter's list of notorious criminals with that of Jude's discloses a functional unity within the longer document. The first three (the sinful angels, the generation at the time of the Flood, and the residents of the Cities of the Plain) project the certainty of divine judgment, with ultimate retribution for rebellious scoffers and with affirmation of the moral loyalists. The fourth, Balaam, is cited between two excoriations (vv. 12–14 and 17–22) of the type of persons who are disrupting the Christian community and whose behavior is in sharp contrast with that which is described in the authoritative words of "the *holy* prophets and the commandment of the Lord and Savior, derived from *your* apostles" (3:2).

SPECIAL PROBLEMS

The history of interpretation reveals that, to say the least, at four points in the text of 2 Peter interpreters have encountered special difficulty. The first of these includes the syntactical relationship of 1:3–5 to the verses that precede and follow. I have suggested that the civic-decree form and its associated diction largely account for the syntactical peculiarity. The second is at 1:19, but it is probable that the understanding of Jesus as Supreme Benefactor, and endorsed by the heavenly voice, leads to the affirmation of v. 19, that the prophetic word is now even more firmly established. The third is at 3:6, in which the phrase *di' hōn* ("through which") must certainly refer to the waters above and those beneath the level of the earth. The fourth, and the most notorious, is found at 3:10.

A number of conjectures have been offered for the last part of v. 10, which the RSV renders: "and the earth and the works that are upon it will be burned up." The New English Bible reads: "and the earth with all that is in it will be laid bare." The question is whether, with NEB, the word *heurethēsetai* is to be read or, with RSV, some word meaning "burned up" or "destroyed." A simple emendation, however, will account for the apparently more difficult verb *heuriskomai* and yet assign it a more probable syntactical usage.

It should be noted, first of all, that the conjunction *kai* after the word *gē* is suspect and may well have been written very early by mistake in place of the original writer's probable *kata*. Manuscript Alexandrinus actually contains such a mistake, reading *kai* instead of *kata* just before the phrase *to epaggelma autou* ("his promise"), in v. 13. If *kata* is to be read also in v. 10, then we should also remember that *gē* written in uncial script could be either dative or nominative case. Since the iota subscript to indicate the dative for the noun *gē* would not be expected in the uncial script, a copyist in the very earliest stages of transmission of 2 Peter might have thought that both the nouns *gē* (earth) and *erga* (works) were nominatives and naturally to be joined by *kai*, instead of *kata*, with *ta* in *kata* easily bypassed because of the following article *ta*. Therefore in place of *kai gē* (nominative) *kai ta en autē erga heurethēsetai*, we propose
kai gē (dative)   *kata ta en autē erga heurethēsetai*. Once the copyist had made this simple mistake, understanding *gē* to be nominative and writing *kai ta* instead of *kata ta*, then the natural use of *heurethēsetai* with the dative in the legal sense "it will be found to so and so," meaning "so and so will be judged," was obscured. Thus the door was opened for the introduction of other variants. In Pss. of Sol. 17:10, a pseudepigraphical work emanating from Pharasaic circles around the first century, the judicial denotation of *heuriskesthai* occurs with both a dative and the preposition *kata: heurethēnai autois kata ta erga autōn*, meaning "they will be judged according to their works." The reconstructed text of 2 Pet. 3:10 (*kai gē kata ta en autē erga heurethēsetai*) contains parallel phraseology, rendered literally: "And it will be found to the earth according to the works in it," that is, "And the earth will be judged according to the works in it." The term "earth" is here applied to its inhabitants, as in Matt. 5:13; 10:34; Luke 12:49, 51.

THE LETTER OF JUDE

Jude has not exactly been a household word among preachers and scholars, and the reasons are rather obvious. It is a highly polemical writing with a low kerygmatic profile. The best part of it is the doxology which closes the letter.

But is it a letter? It begins with a prescript, but ends without epistolary conclusion (cf. 2 Clement). It is addressed to all Christians rather than to specific communities. However, the situation which prompted its writing was specific, namely, the inroads made by heretics into a community within the author's own context. By putting his tract into the form of a letter addressed to all Christians the author, whom we will continue to call Jude, intended to give an ecumenical, catholic dimension to his own struggle against the heretics.

Who were those heretics? It is not easy to get a picture of them from Jude nor can we identify them with any of the heretical groups of the second century which we know, much less is it possible to get a fair picture—as they would have presented themselves. Moreover, we should keep in mind that accusations of fornication, homosexuality (cf. vv. 6–8), flattery (v. 16), gluttony (v. 12), greediness (vv. 11b, 16), godlessness (v. 15), ignorance (v. 10), etc. were standard features of polemics in antiquity generally and were also used in Christian polemics. (Cf. W. Bauer, XXIII, pp. 38 f., 133–146.) On the other hand, had Jude's opponents been paragons of virtue his blast against them would surely have backfired within his own historical context and his appeal to join the fight for the "most holy faith" (3, 20) would have had no basis at all. We hear from Jude that "some" heretics had stealthily slipped into Christian communities from elsewhere and had gained considerable influence (4, 12, 23). Orthodox writers liked to portray heretics as coming from outside the community, not as originating from within. (Cf. Ignatius, Eph. 9:1; W. Bauer, p. 83.) Itinerant preachers were also a common feature of the ecclesiastical landscape of early Christianity and hence Jude v. 4 may well be right.

At any rate, these persons claimed to be Christians. They participate in the agape meals (v. 12), and therefore are accepted by the members of the church. These "love feasts" are still regular meals (cf. the verbs of v. 12) in the context of which the eucharist was celebrated. In Jude's community the Lord's Supper had not yet been separated from the regular meal (cf. 1 Cor. 11:20–22, 25, 33 f.). The verb *poimainō* (I shepherd) in v. 12 probably also indicates that they regarded themselves, or were regarded by others, as shepherds of true Christians.

On the basis of v. 19 we may conclude that Jude's opponents appear to be Gnostic Christians who "make distinctions" between "psychic persons, devoid of the Spirit" and the pneumatics, whose divine *pneuma* spark cannot be destroyed by anything—including God's judgment. *Apodiorizontes* (v. 19) does not indicate schisms which have fragmented the community already. After all, these people participate in the community's agape. It rather refers to the opponents' distinction between members who merely believe the church's tradition and the "true" pneumatics who know "true" freedom (cf. 1 Cor. 2:13 ff.; Irenacus, Haer. I: 6:2 f.; 25:4). Jude turned his opponents' distinctions against them in v. 19.

His opponents have "visions" or "dreams," that is, they claim to be the recipients of new, supernatural revelation (v. 8). For Jude these dreamers are false prophets (cf. Deut. 13:1–5; Isa. 56:10; Jer. 27:9), yet they themselves may have claimed to stand within the tradition of Christian enthusiasm promised by Joel 2:28 and fulfilled in Acts 2:27. As ecstatic visionaries, rather than as wishful dreamers, they undergirded their teaching and lifestyle with their revelations (cf. Col. 2:18).

Jude denounced the teaching of these heretics severely. What "they have spoken" (v. 15b) are *hyperogka* (v. 16b), "high sounding things." Part of their teaching is that they "revile" the authority of angels (v. 8c). These "glorious ones" represent the law and order of God (cf. Acts 7:53; Heb. 2:2; Gal. 3:19; 4:3; Col. 2:14–15). But they also "set aside the Lordship" of God (v. 8b). They understand themselves to be superior to angelic powers and what they represent, and hence they "blaspheme" them in word and deed. Jude's description of the heretics as "grumblers, dissatisfied with fate" (v. 16) may well reflect their dualistic ideology which issued in a negative attitude toward creation, an attitude which is offset by their Gnostic superiority complex. Their contempt for angels and moral law is the consequence of their Gnostic self-understanding.

Their heresy becomes visible to Jude in their libertinistic lifestyle, which to them is undoubtedly the manifestation of their freedom. Sexual licentiousness and perversion are its outstanding but not exclusive features (vv. 4, 7–8, etc.). They "pervert God's grace" into freedom for wantonness and they "deny the only master" (probably God) "and our Lord Jesus Christ" (v. 4). The doctrine of God's future judgment is either irrelevant to them or rejected by them. Jude holds it to be a shame that these "blemishes" (or "reefs beneath the surface of the sea") participate in the sacrament (v. 12).

How did Jude argue with the heretics? He did not—he merely denounced them.

They are not Gnostics or pneumatics at all (v. 19), but sheer animals (v. 10) with instincts based on sex and food, on greed and obstinacy. Woe to those followers of Cain, Balaam, and Korah who go to hell (vv. 11–13), as prophesied (vv. 14–16). The Greek text of vv. 22–23 is no longer clear, but the final injunction, which is without a variant reading, demands that believers "hate even a (heretic's) garment spotted by the flesh" (v. 23). What does that mean? Jude would not agree that clothes make the man. It may be that for him what a man really is is transmitted by his clothing. Holiness or immorality become contagious via garments. This quasi-magical notion is also present in Mark 5:27–30 and Acts 18:12. If so, Jude's injunction would demand a separation from heretics, lest believers be defiled by the immorality emitted even from their garments.

A slightly different approach, which reaches the same conclusion, would see in this clause (v. 23b) Jude turning the language of his opponents against them. To them "the garment" meant the true pneumatic self. For Jude it means the old self which is to be put off (cf. Rev. 3:4; Rom. 13:12). A new self is to be put on (Rev. 3:5; Rom. 13:14; Gal. 3:27; Eph. 4:22–24). At any rate, "hating" the old self of the heretics demands total separation from them (cf. 2 John v. 10). The phrase "Have mercy on some with fear" (v. 23), if original, may imply intercessory prayers in their behalf that they may put on a new garment which is in agreement with the faith delivered unto the saints.

Jude does not argue this point; he merely denounces his opponents in contrast to Paul who, faced with the practice of immorality, developed a series of arguments in order to *persuade* (e.g., 1 Corinthians 6).

Perhaps Jude had become tired of trying to persuade them and all that was left for him to do was to indict the heretics, painting them with the colors of the damned, and to call his troops to battle, admonishing them to hold fast to the true tradition. His was not Ignatius' call: Submit to the bishop and you submit to Christ (Tralles 2; Ephesians 5; Smyrna 8). Perhaps the bishops in Jude's situation had failed to eliminate the heretics from the Christian love feasts, a possibility which Ignatius had apparently not foreseen. In any case, Jude issued his admonition without making direct references to the established ecclesiastical office. His weapon is not the office as such, but "the faith delivered once and for all unto the saints." This is the infallible and immutable divine tradition which the Spirit "delivered" once and for all times to the apostles, and which was transmitted to subsequent generations. The succession of tradition, rather than the succession of apostolically ordained ecclesiastical functionaries is the basis on which Jude made his appeal and gave his indictment. For Jude as for the Pastorals, the ministerial office still stands in the service of the word-become-tradition, and not vice versa, i.e., the tradition does not yet legitimize and serve the office.

In Jude faith is neither personal trust in God's promise enacted in the Christ event, nor is it the eschatological time of salvation breaking into the present, liberating from the slavery and curse of the law (e.g., Gal. 3:23). It is *fides quae*, the tradition which is to be believed (v. 3). Paul also used traditions to orient the faith (1 Cor. 15:1–5) and the Johannine christological dogma (cf. John 16: 27b–28) likewise is *fides quae creditur*. However, in neither case is faith the sum total of immutable traditions. This faith is presented by Jude as the true Gnosis. Those to whom it has been transmitted "know all things once and for all" (v. 5, in distinction to 1 Cor. 13:9). This expresses not merely conventional epistolary politeness (cf. 1 Thess. 4:9; Rom. 15:14) but the conviction that the orthodox tradition mediates the true Gnosis (cf. 1 John 2:21, 27). Accordingly, what is new is not true and what is true is not new, but part of the "faith delivered once and for all unto the saints."

We do not know the content of Jude's tradition, which he calls

"faith" except that it certainly included extra-canonical traditions
found in the Assumption of Moses and 1 Enoch. One example will
have to suffice. According to v. 4 the godless *palai progegrammenoi*
have long ago been inscribed, marked down in heavenly books or
tablets as persons destined for judgment. (For the idea of heavenly
tablets see: Jub. 5:13–14; 1 Enoch 81:1–2; 106:19; 108:7; Test.
Asher 7:5 [Riessler ed., 1928, p. 1231].)

Extra-canonical Jewish traditions are present also in v. 6 (1 Enoch,
chap. 6–7; 10–13; 12:4); in v. 7 (the Sodomites "went after other
flesh" means that they fornicated with angels, contrary to Genesis 19,
where they tried but did not succeed. For the location of the "eternal
fire" see Wis. 10:6–7); in v. 9 (Clement of Alexandria G.C.S. III, 207
refers to the Assumption of Moses which survived only in fragments);
in v. 11 (cf. Test. Benjam. 7:5; *NTS* 5, 1958, 45–47); in v. 12 (cf.
Assump. Moses 7:3–5; for the apocalyptic notion of moral chaos as
sign of the End, see 1 Enoch 91:6–7; for examples from nature see 1
Enoch 2:1–5:4); in vv. 14–16 (cf. 1 Enoch 1:9; 93:3; 5:4).

1 Enoch with its prophecies of the heretics' fate (vv. 14 f.) is just
as much a part of Jude's "faith" as are "the predictions of the
apostles of our Lord" (v. 17), concerning the appearance of heretics
in the last days before the End (cf. Assump. Moses 7; Mark 13:6,
22; 1 John 2:18–19). Tertullian therefore wanted to include 1
Enoch in the canon, while others of the third century wanted to exclude Jude. Already 2 Peter, which used Jude as a source, had
omitted the references to Enoch (Jude v. 14) and to the Assumption of Moses (Jude v. 9). Jude's post-apostolic pseudonymous
character (v. 19 and "the faith" in v. 3) as well as its literary relationship to 2 Peter were recognized by Luther also (W.A., Bibel VII,
p. 384).

The purpose of Jude's invective against the heretics was to warn
his people that apostasy is followed by condemnation. "He (Jesus?)
who saved a people out of the land of Egypt afterward destroyed
those who did not believe" (v. 5; cf. 1 Cor. 10:3–5). Note that
also for Jude the believers are the people of God just as in 1 Peter or
Hebrews. Hence his ecclesiology is not a characteristic of a "Petrine
school." Also note the discussion above on second repentance in
Hebrews. Jude v. 5 is in essential agreement with Heb. 6:4–6.
Jude's central admonition to his readers follows from his warning in

v. 5. "Keep yourselves in the love of God" (v. 21). This aorist imperative is explicated by three present participles (vv. 20–21). To keep oneself in God's love means first of all to build oneself up on the foundation of the tradition (v. 20; cf. Eph. 2:20) which is "most holy" because it comes from God and has been delivered once and for all to God's holy ones (v. 3). This tradition has taken the place of the Torah. Second, to keep oneself in God's love demands prayer "in the Holy Spirit" (v. 20; cf. Eph. 6:18; Rom. 8:26–27). It is possible that the Gnostics in Jude's community rejected prayer altogether. In the Gospel according to Thomas, log. 14, we read: "If you pray you will be condemned" (cf. log. 16). At any rate, for Jude the Gnostics cannot pray in the Spirit because they "do not have the Spirit" (v. 19). The Spirit which is necessary for prayer is bound up with the tradition. Third, to keep oneself in God's love means to "wait for the mercy of our Lord Jesus Christ" who at his parousia will lead the faithful into eternal life (v. 21). Note the proto-trinitarian thought in these verses. Until the eschaton "the only God our Savior through Jesus Christ" is able to "keep you from falling and to present you without blemish before his presence" (vv. 24–25)—provided you keep yourselves in his love (vv. 20–21).

As a writer Jude was fond of producing triads and triple arrangements. For example, in v. 1 Christians are described as "called, beloved . . . and kept"; in v. 2 we have mercy, peace, love; in v. 4 the godless are "inscribed . . . they pervert . . . they deny"; in vv. 5–7 there are three OT examples; see also vv. 8, 11–12, 19, and perhaps 22–23. He used stylized invective in vv. 12, 16, 19. Two types occur, one with predicate nouns, the other with participles. Both styles are found in apocalyptic literature not only for revealing and denouncing the godless (e.g., Slav. Enoch 7:3) but also for praising God and the righteous (1 Enoch 46:3; Rev. 7:14; Acts 7:35). V. 15 is carefully balanced (a-b-b1-b2); v. 16 is in the form of parallelism. Prophetic aorists are found in vv. 11 and 14 and there are still other literary techniques in this brief writing, especially in vv. 12–13.

The question of the value of Jude for today's preacher must at last be raised and faced. Jude brings up the problem of the canon, both of the NT and OT, and testifies to the canon's relativity. Moreover, Jude raises the problem of polemics, its importance, its necessity, and its dangers. A few comments: From Genesis to the Apocalypse the

Bible is also a polemical book. Moses and the prophets, Jesus and the apostles, the evangelists and the pseudonymous NT authors also engaged in polemics. The preacher who can no longer say this or that is wrong has forfeited the authority to say what is right. Polemics is implicit in every confession of faith. Moreover, the situation may arise where pure polemics such as that practiced by Jude is the most effective way of proclaiming the word of God and of recalling the people of the church to the "faith delivered once and for all to the saints" to which the NT in the plurality of its witnesses bears witness. As a teenager in Germany I heard one particular sermon, a pure denunciation of the idolatry of the Nazi religion of "blood and land," of Moloch worship and the hatred of Cain. It was not based on Jude, but it made a lasting impression. The enemy then, as in Jude's situation, was also the compromiser and synthesizer within the church.

However, most situations don't present us with clear cut alternatives, but with various shades of gray. Polemics itself becomes demonic the moment the preacher loves it, venting his spleen, riding his hobby horse, putting people down for the sheer fun of it, and imagining that he speaks for God. Since time and again teachers and preachers have engaged in polemics for the wrong reason (e.g., the earth is flat and the Bible is inerrant in every historical detail) and at the wrong occasion (e.g., when God's grace and Christ's Lordship were not really at stake but rather the preacher's myopic view of them) it may be just as well that Jude has not become a household word.

THE REVELATION TO JOHN

The church father Jerome expressed in a letter to the bishop Paulinus of Nola his great difficulties in understanding Revelation: "The Apocalypse of John has as many secrets as words" (Ep. LIII. 9). Likewise for many contemporary Christians, preachers, and theologians, Revelation appears to be an ancient puzzle whose meaning is lost forever. Other Christians find in it exact predictions of the end of the world, and the events which must happen beforehand. They misuse the book as a time-schedule for the last days to which they alone have the right key.

Many have not only characterized the book as bizarre and unintelligible but have also labeled it as sub- or unchristian, full of divine revenge and fierce wrath and lacking the proclamation of God's love and grace. Many preachers and commentators never refer to the book because they agree with Martin Luther's verdict: "My spirit cannot accommodate itself to this book. There is one sufficient reason for the small esteem in which I hold it—that Christ is neither taught in it nor recognized."

INTRODUCTION

One receives quite a different impression of the book when one attempts to analyze and determine the content of the book or when one listens to the book in its totality as one would listen to a symphony or poem. It is almost impossible to interpret the images and symbols of Revelation in a definite way or to define its theological contents with certainty. The text of Revelation presents repetitions, doublets, and artificial constructions. The logical flow of thought and the temporal sequence of the visions appear to be repetitive and disturbed, the sense of time and development confused, and the images and symbols often arbitrary and obscure. Scholars have attempted to explain the doublets, inconsistencies, or incongruities of the text either as being due to the faulty memory of the author who wrote the book at lengthy intervals or they have postulated that the author died and an incompetent student then edited the whole work with insufficient sensitivity and understanding.

Source critical analyses attempt to order the narrative in such a way that it represents a logical, linear, and unified theological system. They single out and separate as traditional those elements which either destroy the logical or temporal sequence and contradict its main symbols or do not agree with what is preconceived as the central Christian theological statement of the book. They have often understood Revelation to be basically a Jewish writing to which Christian corrections and insertions have been added.

Today the source-theories of the last century have widely been relinquished and replaced by the scholarly consensus that Revelation is the theological work of an author who used different sources and traditions to express his own vision. Whereas the various source-theories assumed that Revelation is a more or less mechanical compilation of heterogeneous sources, scholars today argue that the book is a work of carefully planned organization and artistic composition. Against the arbitrary dissection of Revelation into various sources stands the unitary character of the language and symbol system of the book. We can, therefore, attribute the overall plan and theological intention of the book to one single author but account for its inconsistencies and discrepancies by assuming that the author incorporated various oral or written traditions into the composition of his work. He has done this in such a skillful way that the book now mirrors his theological vision and literary composition. This view takes into account the unity of Revelation as well as the discrepant materials which seemingly do not fit into their present context. In order to understand the book we have first to elucidate the overall meaning and structure which the author has intended. Knowing his traditions and sources helps us to work out a clearer profile of his thought but it cannot explain the overall composition and theological focus of the book.

The author's compositional procedure, however, presents one of the main difficulties for the interpretation of the book. Since the author does not quote but paraphrases his materials or only alludes to them, as can clearly be seen from his employment of OT texts, it is very difficult to separate tradition from redaction or to give a definite meaning to the images and symbols of the book. The multivalent character of the imagery of Revelation is often due to heterogeneous traditions pressed into a new framework of composition. Revelation appears therefore on the one hand as an artificial construction of different materials derived from traditions which are heterogeneous in origin and theology, and impresses one on the other hand as an artistic mosaic of poetical conciseness.

The artistic, poetic character of Revelation can best be experienced when one hears the book read aloud in its entirety. The hearer of the text in its totality is impressed by its archaic and rhythmic language, by its repetition of sounds and formulas, by the wealth of its colors, voices, symbols, and image-associations. Due to its wholeness of expression and unitary character of language Revelation is the one book of the NT which has received the attention of artists throughout the centuries and has inspired great works of art, music, and literature. It may be difficult for the pictorial painter to reproduce the almost surrealistic symbols and bizarre images of the book, whereas the modern artist might appreciate its colors and forms. Modern literature derives many of its motifs and stylistic elements from the book. The visions of the "new land" and the "New Jerusalem" resonate in the music and poetry of oppressed people. This poetic and dramatic character of the book can be best perceived when the text is read aloud as the author intended it to be.

We ought therefore not overlook the fact that the dramatic and symbolic character of Revelation defies exact analysis and fixed interpretation. The author did not write a tractate or essay on the "last things" but intended to stun us with the power of his images and visions. The images and symbols of the book have evocative character. They not only provoke an intellectual response, but they also elicit an emotional reaction.

If we are patient enough to study Revelation on its own terms we might be able to participate in the theological vision of the author which he developed not in abstract sentences but in the language of symbol and myth. It would therefore be a serious mistake to view Revelation as a logical system or a theological argument. We have to approach the book in the same manner in which we approach a work of art. In hearing a symphony, for example, we have first to listen to the whole work in order to grasp the full impact of its total composition, its tonal colors, musical forms, its motifs and relationships. Yet after we have listened again and again to the work as a whole we have to go on to analyze the elements and details of its composition and to study the techniques employed by the composer. We have to compare it with other works of the same period and have to listen to different interpretations of it. All this does not mean that we can exactly pinpoint the thought of its composer, but we will achieve a deeper *understanding* of this particular work of music.

The same holds true for studying the Book of Revelation. Whereas only the patient hearing and reading of the book as a whole can transmit a total impression of its vision and perspective, a careful and detailed analysis of various aspects of the book might enhance our comprehension and interpretation.

THE STRUCTURE AND COMPOSITION OF REVELATION

The quality and impact of a literary work depends on how well the author interrelates its content and form of expression. In order to understand a literary work we have therefore not only to know its content but also to observe how the author expressed and formulated it. The same experience and truth can be expressed in different modes. A poem or drama, a novel or short story, a slogan or advertisement formulate the same insight and truth in different ways. The same is true for the understanding of biblical literature. The message about Jesus Christ receives a different *gestalt* in a gospel, a letter, or a homily. Any interpretation of Revelation has therefore to ask not only the difficult question: "What did the author want to say?" but also "How did he express it?" If we are able to determine the form and the structure of a work, we are more likely to be able to interpret its different sections and images more correctly. The rhetoric of a poem is different from that of a novel, and that of an advertisement different from that of a joke. It would therefore be of great importance for the theological understanding of Revelation if we could rediscover the structuring and organizing principle as well as the compositional method which the author employed in writing the book. The manifold solutions which scholars have suggested to the problem indicate that it is no longer possible to answer this question with certainty. The following attempt to order the contents of the book and to determine its compositional means must therefore remain hypothetical but might prove helpful to gain an overall view of the work.

The Plan and Structure of Revelation

The introduction of the book which is patterned after the introduction of OT prophetic books spells out the main content of Revelation. It represents a "revelation (apocalypse) of Jesus Christ" to John who is to communicate it to seven named communities of Asia Minor. The author instructs his readers that the book should be read aloud at the gathering of the community (1:1–3). In vv. 4 f. follows an epistolary address, and in vv. 7–8 the theme of Revelation consisting of an announcement of the parousia and a direct word of God.

The Structural Units of Revelation

1:9–3:22 form the first section of Revelation. The seven letters are prophetic address of the resurrected Lord to the communities. It is also clear that the visions of the eschatological salvation are a unit of their own. This last unit begins with the parousia-vision in Rev. 19:11 and ends with the prophetic promise in 22:5. The main part of the book extends from 4:1–19:10. There is much discussion about how this main part is to be subdivided. However, it is interesting to note that Revelation 4–5 and Revelation 10 represent two commissioning visions in which "scrolls" play the key role.

Since the seven seal visions (6:1–8:1) are formally linked with the inaugural vision of chapters 4–5 on the one hand and with the two following plague septets, on the other hand, we can assume that the three septet visions belong together in the mind of the author. The trumpet (8:2–9:21; 11:15–19) and the bowl (15:1, 5–16:21) septet present formally and contentually a development of the seal-septet. Since the so-called Babylon visions 17:1–19:10 are an extension of the bowl-septet (cf. 17:1) as well as an anti-image to the New Jerusalem (21:9), they form a transitional unit to the last part of Revelation. Between the septet of the trumpets and that of the bowls the author has inserted 10:1–15:4. The content of the small scroll which is seen as parallel to the seven-sealed scroll, is characterized in the commissioning vision of chapter 10 as "prophetic word." The three plague septets of the "sealed scroll" thus represent a literary unit which encloses the "prophetic scroll" (10:1–15:4).

The seven pattern of the plagues appears to be determinative for the structure of the book. It also links the main part of the book to the beginning unit of the letters which shows the same seven structure. The author manifests his structural intention by placing the seven letters on one level with the seven visions of the plagues insofar as, on the one hand, he characterizes the letters together with the inaugural vision (1:10–20) as one great, unified vision, and on the other hand he intertwines by means of the insertion of the "small scroll" the cosmic septets with the fate of the community on earth. Moreover, the first section of the book is related to the last unit insofar as the promises to the victorious in the seven letters are all taken up again in the last part of the book and the figure of the parousia-Christ in 19:11–16 resembles features of the Christ figure of 1:12–20.

Contentual Analysis

A summary analysis of the content of these four main parts of Revelation can highlight their major themes and theological intention.

The *seven prophetic-apocalyptic letters* (1:9–3:22) are revelations and proclamations by the risen Christ to the churches in Asia Minor. They give a stylized, but not idealized description of the communities insofar as the author points out their strengths and weaknesses. His main objective is prophetical exhortation, critical evaluation, and strengthening encouragement. On the whole the author places strong emphasis on the works or praxis of the communities. Yet not all the churches are still doing "the works of their first love." Some do not reject the message of rival teachers, others are no longer "alive" and are even in danger of being "cast away." His main exhortation is therefore to encourage them to remember what Christ has done for them, to repent and to endure, to hold fast to what they have. These admonitions indicate that these communities of Asia Minor are not newly founded but appear to have existed already for a long time. They are threatened by rival Christian teachers, by those who call themselves Jews, and by the Roman civil religion. The power behind this threefold threat in the author's view

is Satan (cf. 2:10, 12, 24).   All the letters close with an admonition
to hear "what the Spirit says" and the eschatological promise to those
who will be victorious.   The constant factors of the letters are first,
the prophetic messenger formula and the emphasis on Christ's knowledge of the community, and second, the call to listen and the eschatological promise to the victorious.   It is interesting to note that these
prophetic-apocalyptic letters of the risen Christ uttered through the
Spirit take the same place within the composition of Revelation which
in Jewish apocalypses is often given to the survey of history.

The *seven-sealed scroll unit (4:1–19:10)* is introduced by a
double inaugural vision in chapters 4 and 5.   Chapter 4 presents the
heavenly courtroom with God as a great king sitting on the throne.
The concluding two hymns praise God as Creator and celebrate
God's holiness and power.   Both chapters are full of liturgical symbols (altar, incense, torches, priestly elders, hymns, etc.), but the
author employs these liturgically shaped materials and setting to un-
derline God's and Christ's kingly power and universal judgment over
the world.

The object of chapter 5 is the commissioning of the slain Lamb
who alone is worthy to receive and open the seven-sealed scroll.   The
contents of the scroll are clearly the eschatological judgments and
catastrophes portrayed in the three plague septets and set in motion
by the loosening of the seals.   By taking possession of the scroll the
Lamb is enthroned as the eschatological ruler of the world who is to
execute the plagues of the End-time on the world.   The three plague
septets portray this execution of his eschatological rule and judgment.
Whereas the visions of the seals report the events traditionally
expected in the End-time (anti-Christ, war, hunger, death, cf. Mark
13), the septets of the bowls and trumpets picture God's day of wrath
in cosmic catastrophes as the new exodus of the people of God from
the oppression of the present world-powers.   The sequence of the
plagues is therefore not chronological-temporal, but follows a certain
pattern and topology of eschatological events.   All three septets refer
to the same events of the End-time.   But whereas the trumpet
plagues strike only a third of the cosmos and of humanity, the septet
of the bowls of wrath destroys the whole world.

The content of the *small scroll (10:1–15:4)* has been inserted
between the visions of the trumpets and bowls as a "prophetic word"

interpreting the situation of the Christians in the End-time. The two commissioning visions in 10:1–11:2 direct our attention from the cosmic-heavenly realm to what is happening on earth. The author is told to "prophesy" about "many peoples and nations and tongues" and to "measure" the temple and true worshipers of God. The essential content of the "small scroll" is sketched in the vision of the "two prophetic 'witnesses" and unfolded from a different perspective in chapters 12–15. While actions of the three septets of the plagues are of cosmic-universal nature, the main function of the "small scroll" is the prophetic interpretation of the situation of the persecuted Christians. The author links chapters 11, 12, and 13 by means of the main figure "the beast" and of the Danielic phrase "a time and times and half a time," 42 months, the equivalent of 1260 days.

All visions of the "small scroll" refer to the same time as the eschatological time of tribulation and of probation for the Christian community. This is the time which is given to Satan and his allies who stand behind the persecution of the Christians through the world power Rome. Satan's power is made manifest in the actions of the beast and the false prophet. Features of the Danielic beasts as well as the notion of the anti-Christ have influenced the description of the beast from the abyss. It is a caricature of the Lamb (13:3, 12, 14). As such it is characterized with royal features and its main goal is to seduce people to adore the dragon Satan (13:4). For this purpose it employs the beast from the land, the false prophet who works great signs and miracles to seduce the dwellers on the earth to worship the first beast and its image.

The second beast persecutes and financially boycotts all those who do not accept the mark of the first beast and do not become its worshipers. These characterizations of the satanic powers, according to most exegetes, suggest a personification of the political and religious leaders of the Roman empire and especially appear to refer to the imperial cult. The Christians are called to resist these powers which presently usurp the rule and honor of God and Christ on earth. They are admonished to choose captivity and death over the idolatrous worship of the Roman civil religion (13:9 f). The prophetic scroll-unit climaxes in the eschatological victory song of those "who have conquered the beast and its image and the number of its

name" (15:2). The prophetic message demands unwavering resis-
ance to the anti-divine, satanic, and political powers.

By making the "small scroll" unit the formal center of Revelation,
the author underlines the central theme and objective of the whole
book. It seeks to interpret prophetically the situations of the Christians in Asia Minor in the "short time" before the End. Christ has
won the final victory, he is the true ruler of the world, and exercises
his ruling power over the world in the cosmic, eschatological plagues.
The Christians have not yet won the victory. They are still immersed
in the power struggle between the divine and the satanic reign and
kingdom. For a short time the anti-divine powers appear to win out
and to reign on earth. The main part of Revelation therefore describes in mythological language the threat of the religious and political powers against the Christians who are the representatives of
God's kingdom on earth. Their suffering and oppression calls out for
the final coming of Christ to restore justice and to establish the rule
also on earth which he exercises now in heaven.

Just as the various cycles of visions throughout the book do, so too
does Revelation as a whole climax in the visions of *judgment and
salvation* (19:11–22:5). The destruction of the satanic powers is
described in the reverse order of their introduction in chapters 12–14.
The judgment of Babylon and its followers is followed by the
judgment over the beast and false prophet, over the dragon, and over
Hades and Death. Only then will the last judgment take place
(20:11–15). The whole cosmos (heaven, earth, and underworld)
is thereby torn away from the satanic powers and placed under the
rule of God. Whereas the septets of plagues describe the End as the
"day" of God's wrath, the visions of judgment at the end of the book
emphasize the liberation of the earth from the satanic powers and the
establishment of God's and Christ's reign on a new earth in the New
Jerusalem. The reign of God and Christ which is symbolized in the
presence of the throne in the New Jerusalem means freedom from
oppression, suffering, and death. It means participation in the reign
of Christ and God, and living in their presence.

The final section of the book takes up all the eschatological promises of the seven prophetic-apocalyptic letters and describes them as
fulfilled. This section of Revelation ends with the blessing of Moses

which is followed by the promise: "They shall reign forever and ever" (22:3–5). This promise recalls the last promise of the seven letters: "He who conquers, I will grant him to sit with me on my throne, as I myself conquered and sat down with my Father on his throne" (3:21).

Conclusion

The composition of Revelation builds a bridge from the "now" of the Christian communities to that of the eschatological future when all the anti-divine and dehumanizing powers will be destroyed. The first section of the seven letters looks at the churches standing under the judgment and protection of their Lord. In 19:11–22:5 the author sketches the liberation of the world from all evil powers and the salvation of the New Jerusalem, the universal community on the New Earth. The prophetic interpretation of the present persecution of the Christians as the last time before the End represents the center of the composition. The eschatological cosmic plagues, the description of the day of God's wrath, and the judgment and destruction of the dehumanizing power of Rome, its idolatry and the satanic powers behind it, occupy the largest part of the book. We ought, however, not to overlook that the author does not posit an absolute dualism between the Christians and "the dwellers of the earth." Not only the seven letters but the whole book are full of ethical admonitions and exhortations for the Christians. This ethical interest of the author prevents the reader of that time as well as us from projecting "evil" only unto others but not to hold ourselves accountable. Revelation speaks not only of vengeance against the dehumanizing, anti-Christian, demonic, and political powers, but also calls the inhabitants of the earth as well as the Christians to repentance. The author insists that the Christians in no way have "made it" but that they are still in danger of losing their share in the New Jerusalem. The Book of Revelation could easily be misunderstood in the sense that "evil" exists only outside the Christian community but not within it if the author had not taken care to begin with the great vision of the heavenly Christ judging the Christian communities, to intersperse the cosmic-apocalyptic part with eschatological warnings, blessings, exhortations, and woes, and to conclude the whole book with a series of admonitions, announcements, and prayers (22:6–21).

Means of Composition

The analysis of the structure and plan of Revelation indicates that the author did not develop it in a linear-temporal fashion, but in a topical-thematical way. The movement of thought and symbols in Revelation does not follow a temporal-logical or temporal-linear plan but can best be envisioned as a conic spiral moving forward in broken cycles to the climax of the book in the visions of eschatological salvation. The development of thought is not chronological-logical but could be likened to a musical theme or motif with variations, each variation moving and enhancing the total composition.

Since we are used to a linear-logical development of thought or a linear-temporal sequence of narrated events, it is hard for the modern reader to comprehend the outline and plan of Revelation.   The author achieves this composition by combining the techniques of inclusion or intercalation, of interlacing or interweaving, and by the repetition of the numerical seven pattern.   The whole book is constructed according to the pattern of *inclusion* since the author inserts into an epistolary framework the visions and auditions of Revelation. The method of *intercalation* is employed by the author in the following way: He narrates in two episodes or formally similar units (A and A) what formally or contentually belongs together. Between these two episodes or forms he intercalates another scene or form (B) and thus requires the reader to see the combined text as a unique whole. For example: The author patterns the beginning of Revelation after the introduction of OT prophetic books. The prophetic introduction consists of a superscription (A; cf. 1:1–3) and a motto (A'; cf. 1:7–8). Between the two sections of the prophetic introduction the author inserts the epistolary prescript (B; cf. 1:4–6). The same technique can be employed to construct larger units. Between the Babylon visions in 17:1–19:10 (A) and the Jerusalem visions in 21:9–22:5 (A') is inserted the parousia-judgment series in 19:11–21:9 (B). A variation of this method is the technique of the *interlacing or interweaving* of visions and visionary series. Whereas we are used to *dividing* an outline or plan into sections the author *joins* the various units through interlacing them with each other. We have therefore to pay attention not so much to possible markers of division but to the *joints* in the compositional plan of

Revelation. Such a *joint–unit* is, for instance, 10:1–11:14. Like chapter 7 this unit is an interlude of the trumpet septet and at the same time belongs to the prophetic scroll unit 10:1–15:4.

A primary means of the author to achieve an interwoven texture of the whole book is his use of *numbers and numerical structures.* Basic for the understanding of the structure of Revelation are the four septets and the two scroll-visions in chapters 4–5 and 10. The three plague septets are related to each other as prelude, crescendo, and climax, whereas the letter septet points forward to the visions of eschatological salvation. The interweaving of the visions through the seven-structure has the effect of combining a cyclic form of repetition with a forward thrust of the narrative. The composition of Revelation is end–oriented rather than encyclopaedic.

Interludes representing visions and hymns of eschatological salvation (7:1–17; 11:14–19; 12:10; 14:1–5; 15:2–4; 19:1–8; 20:4–6) interrupt the pattern of continuous forward moving narrative and cyclic repetition. Through the insertion of these anticipatory hymns and visions the author expresses in his composition that the eschatological future already informs the present situation. Other means of the author to achieve a unitary structure are the use of a *common stock* of images and symbols, *image-clusters* and *symbol-associations, pre-announcements, contrasts* and *cross-references.*

Another means of composition is the revision and variation of traditional forms and patterns. The author for the most part does not freely create his materials but takes over traditional patterns and materials especially from the OT, apocalypticism, Jewish and pagan mythology, and early Christian traditions. He does not quote or copy his materials and traditions but rather rephrases and revises them to express his own theological vision. This method can clearly be detected in his use of OT and NT traditions and texts. The book appears therefore to many readers as an artificial construction of heterogeneous texts and traditions as well as an artistic mosaic of unitary composition. For the interpretation and understanding of the book, it is therefore important to observe the integrating principle or idea which brings the traditional materials into a new unique form-constellation.

The exact interpretation of such traditional materials is, however, most difficult whenever we do not know the tradition to which the author refers. Instead of focusing on the traditions we must therefore first determine the author's intention and then attempt to locate the traditions. The myth of the queen of heaven with the eternal child in chapter 12 is a case in point. The elements of the myth are: the woman, the child, his birth and ascension, and the dragon. This myth is international and is found in Egypt (Hathor/Isis, Horus, Set/Tryphon), in Babylon (Demkina, Marduk, Tiamat), in Greece (Letho, Apollo, Python), and in Palestine (Sion, Israel, Messiah, Satan/Behemoth/Leviathan). In each of these examples of the myth the dragon seeks the child who is not yet born in order to harm or to kill him. The woman still pregnant is pursued for the child whom she carries. She gives birth with the dragon only a short distance away. However, the child is caught up to heaven and saved from the persecution by the dragon.

Revelation 12 is thus grounded in a realization of pagan hopes for a hero-king and Jewish expectations of the Messiah. In Revelation's theology this child-god is the Christ Jesus. The myth becomes a focus in the composition of the book when one sees that it also has connections with the imperial cult in John's time. The emperor's godliness was perceived as the assumption of the role of the divine child born by the goddess Roma, queen of heaven. If we posit the woman as the queen of heaven, the dragon as the opposing evil forces, then the child is clearly seen as the divine redeemer. Thus the author appeals to associations of very different mythic traditions, but focuses on the divine child, the Messiah and antidote to the divine child born by the goddess Roma. In conclusion: The last example indicates that the author works with patterns of very different traditions and appeals to the imagination of Jews and Hellenists alike. Since, however, the incorporation of very heterogeneous traditions of very different origin tends to disrupt the unitary character of the narrative, the author employs literary techniques and means to integrate the various traditions and symbols into the theological movement of the work. Therefore the Apocalypse does not make an encyclopaedic but a dramatic impression.

INTENTION AND THEOLOGICAL PERSPECTIVE OF REVELATION

The author of the Apocalypse understands his work as an early Christian prophecy and himself as a Christian prophet. He might have been the head of a prophetic school (cf. 22:16). Like the

Hebrew prophets, John takes his standpoint in his own day and age (ca. A.D. 90–96) and does not appeal to ficitional timetables or employ pseudonymity to give his work an authoritative character. His "word of prophecy" is completely committed to the strengthening of the Christian communities in Asia Minor in their severe clash with the anti-divine powers actualized in the Roman state and civil religion. It is therefore no accident that the author patterned the whole book after the then already authoritative pastoral letter form of the Pauline epistles. Like the letters of Paul so too is Revelation directed toward concrete questions and problems of the communities in Asia Minor. As the Pauline epistles situate the problems of the Christian communities in a wider theological context so too does Revelation offer a theological-prophetic interpretation of the concrete situation and problems of these communities.

The Theological Problem

The communities of Asia Minor have already experienced harrassment from the Jews as well as from the Roman authorities, and they have to expect even greater trials, persecutions, and imprisonments. The author seeks to encourage them in their difficult situation by giving a theological meaning to their sufferings and trials. He admonishes them not to avoid prison and death, and not to fall prey to apostasy.

What was the societal and religious position of the Christians in Asia Minor that provoked such a precarious situation? Under the Flavian emperors, Vespasian (69–79), Titus (79–81), and Domitian (81–96), two major developments occurred. First, under the Flavians, especially Domitian, the imperial cult had become increasingly stronger and was especially celebrated in the Roman provinces. Domitian demanded that the populace acclaim him as "Lord and God" and participate in his worship. In the Roman empire such a participation in the state religion was regarded as a sign of political loyalty since the emperor was the living head of the state and its guardian. The Christians who acclaimed Jesus Christ as their "Lord and God" found themselves more and more in difficulties vis à vis the Roman civil religion. Second, the situation was aggravated because the Christians could less and less claim the Jewish privileges for themselves. The Jews of the dispersion had the privilege to practice

their religion in any part of the empire.   They were exempted from
the worship of the emperor and from military service.   Vespasian
ordered that all Jews and proselytes now had to pay a special tax
called the *fiscus Judaicus* to the Romans instead of the tax formerly
paid to the temple.   Domitian enforced the tax and singled out especially the proselytes and God-fearers who were not Jews by birth.
Since moreover through the decisions of Jamnia the Jewish community separated more and more from the Christian church, excluding Jewish Christians from the synagogue, the Christians no longer
could claim the Jewish privileges and often were regarded as disloyal
and atheist.

The letters of Revelation indicate that the Christians in Asia Minor
were exposed to the hostilities of the Jews as well as to those of the
Romans.   It is true that we do not know of a full-fledged persecution
of the Christians before the second century, but the author of Revelation knows of persecutions of individual Christians, and the increas-
ing totalitarianism of the reign of Domitian made the future look
dark.   The everyday experience of harassment and persecutions
stood in glaring contrast to the faith conviction of the Christians.
They proclaimed Jesus Christ as their Lord and King and believed
that they were made in baptism to be members of his kingdom who
already shared in his kingly reign.   Theology and reality contradicted
each other in the concrete experience of the Christians in Asia Minor.
The Christians experienced again and again that their life and
situation in no way reflected their theology of participation in the
kingship and power of Jesus Christ.

This tension between faith-conviction and reality-experience must
have provoked difficult theological questions: Why do Christ's followers have to suffer if Jesus Christ is the true Lord and King of the
world?   Why are the Christians persecuted if God is on their side and
the gods of the other religions are powerless?   If Christ is really the
eschatological regent of God why does he not revenge the blood of so
many Christians who already had to die?   Why did Christ not return
in glory to prevent further suffering of his people?   These pressing
theological queries are given different theological answers by leading
prophets of the churches in Asia Minor.   The author of Revelation
implicitly informs us of this since he argues against a rival prophetic
movement and Christian solution.   This rival prophetic movement

did not represent a heretic Christian group but still lived within the communities.

The Theological Option of the Rival Christian Prophetic Group

The author directly names these rival Christian prophets in the letters to the churches in Ephesus (2:1–7), Pergamum (2:12–17), and Thyatira (2:18–29). Ephesus is praised for rejecting the itinerant apostles of the Nicolaitans, Pergamum is criticized for tolerating them, and Thyatira is censured for accepting the school of a prophet whom the author labels Jezebel. The Nicolaitans or school of Jezebel were probably a libertine enthusiastic Christian group who sought to adapt to their society by eating food sacrificed to idols and by accepting religious syncretism. Insofar as the author likens their teaching to that of Balaam and calls one of their leaders "Jezebel," his further accusation that they committed fornication is probably also meant in a metaphorical sense as practicing syncretism and idolatry.

This stance of the Nicolaitans had great political, economic, and professional advantages for the Christians, for the meat sacrificed to idols was served at the meetings of the trade guilds and business associations as well as at private receptions. Avoidance of idol worship and the imperial cult image was virtually impossible because even the currency one used daily bore the image of the divine emperor. The Nicolaitans' position thus proposed a theological compromise that allowed the Christian citizens of pagan society to participate actively in their city's commercial, social, and political life.

Which theological reasons could the Nicolaitans have given for their advice that the Christians should integrate themselves into their society? What exactly was the theological issue at stake? As the enthusiasts in Corinth had done some forty years earlier so the Nicolaitans probably argued that "idols are nothing" and that therefore the Christians could eat food previously sacrificed to them. Since the Christians, much more than any educated Roman, knew that the Caesar's claim to divinity was nothing else than a constitutional fiction to promote political loyalty to the Roman state, why should they refuse to pay this honor and loyalty to the emperor? Did not the great apostle Paul demand that one submit to the authorities of the state because they were ordained by God (Rom. 13:1–7)? That a Christian of Asia Minor at the end of the first century in the face of suffering (1 Pet. 2:13–17) could argue in such a way is evident from 1 Peter, who admonishes the Christians: "Honor the emperor" (1 Pet. 2:17). Since loyalty to the Roman civil religion did not demand creedal adherence but only participation in the rituals of the imperial cult, it was possible to cultically honor the emperor without relinquishing one's faith in Jesus Christ.

If participation in the ceremonies and rituals of the imperial cult is only an expression of one's political loyalty but does not compromise one's religious faith, it would be foolish to make it a theological issue. To oppose the imperial cult and to risk one's life in opposition to the Roman civil religion would mean to take the sovereignty claims of the emperor and its cult too seriously. The political claim of the emperor and the religious claim of Jesus Christ are not in conflict. The kingship claims of both belong to a radically different order. (For such a distinction cf. John 18:36–38.) Jesus Christ's kingship claims are not of a political nature but pertain to the human soul and the Christian community, since the Christians are taken out of this world and by virtue of their baptism already share in the kingly power and dignity of their Lord (1:5 f.). No one, not even Satan, can harm the elect Christians for they have insight into the very depth of the demonic (2:24) and share in the spiritual community of the divine, heavenly world. If this is the case, why go to prison or die for a cause which is not worthwhile dying for? Is it not true that idols have no real existence (1 Cor. 8:4) and what else is the imperial image than an idol? To say otherwise would be bad theology or religious fanaticism.

The Theological Perspective of Revelation

In responding to the theological challenge of the Nicolaitans the author of Revelation formulates an alternative theological interpretation of the political-religious situation of the Christians in Asia Minor. His answer becomes apparent when we interrelate his sharp rejection of the Nicolaitans in the seven letters with his urgent denunciation of the imperial cult in the apocalyptic visions in the central section of Revelation. His theological response asserts that no coexistence is possible between the kingship claim of God and that of

Caesar, because God and Christ are the true rulers of the world and nations. The conflict between the kingdom of God and Christ on the one hand and that of the beast and Babylon on the other hand is the major theological theme of Revelation and the image and symbol of the throne is its central theological image.

Revelation envisions *God* as the great-king "sitting on the throne" in royal splendor and power surrounded by twenty-four vassal-kings and the heavenly court (chap. 4) who proclaim day and night: "Holy, holy, is the Lord God Almighty" (4:8). God is the king, the pantocrator or all-powerful, because God is the creator of everything, of heaven and earth. God's kingship claim pertains therefore not only to the soul or to the heavenly world, but to everything, to the political-societal realm and to the whole world. God's reign, however, cannot coexist with any dehumanizing power that destroys the earth. God's reign over the earth is therefore established in judgment over the world and over the destroyers of the earth (cf. 11:17 f.). Revelation therefore climaxes with the visions of judgment and of a new creation, a new heaven and earth, where God's dominion over humankind means light, richness, life, and salvation:

> Behold the dwelling of God is with human beings
> God will dwell with them and they shall be God's people
> and God will be with them.
> God will wipe every tear from their eyes,
> and death shall be no more,
> neither shall there be mourning nor crying nor pain any more
> for the former things have passed away. (21:3 f)

Jesus Christ is not only the Lord and judge of his community (1:12–20) but he is the "King of Kings and Lord of Lords" (19:16 cf. 17:14). He shares in the throne and kingly reign of his Father because he was victorious (3:21). The only reference to the life of Jesus is to his death. He is the "first-born of the dead" (1:5), "who died and came to life" (2:8), the slaughtered Lamb who is the Davidic Messiah (5:5). As the exalted one he alone in the whole world is worthy to take over the seven-sealed scroll and with it the eschatological dominion over the world. His universal kingship is based on the fact that he "was slain" and has "ransomed from every tribe and tongue and nation" people whom he has "made to a kingdom and priests for God." They will share in the divine reign on earth in the eschatological future (5:9–10).

Revelation not only professes that Jesus Christ is the Lord and King of the world but also reiterates the early Christian baptismal confession that Christ made the baptized to a kingdom and appointed them as priests (1:6; cf. 5:10). In distinction to the rival prophets of the Nicolaitans the author understands the royal expressions "kingdom, kingship, reign," not in a spiritualistic sense as pertaining only to the individual soul and the heavenly-spiritual realm, but in the tradition of Jewish eschatology he conceives of them as concrete political-societal realities. Since the exalted Lord has taken over the kingship and power over the world in heaven, the Christians are by virtue of their baptism the representatives of God's kingdom and reign on earth and as such the anti-kingdom to the Roman empire with its universal claims. Any acknowledgment of the imperial cult and power denies God's and Christ's claim to divine Lordship over the world and nations. The imperial cult and image are as idols, "nothing," but behind them stands Satan, the anti-divine power par excellence. The power behind the political domination "which corrupts the earth" is the dragon-devil who has come down from heaven (12:12). He gave to the "beast from the sea," the Roman emperor, "his power, his throne, and his great authority" (13:2) which is universal and affects Christians and non-Christians alike:

> also it was allowed to make war on the saints and to conquer them. And authority was given it over every tribe and people and tongue and nation, and all who dwell on earth will worship it . . . (13:7 f.)

Loyalty to the Roman emperor who claims the divine honor and power due to God and Christ, means treason and betrayal of the power and kingdom of God. Rome's absolute claim to divine power and honors forces the either-or situation upon the Christians and the inhabitants of the earth. Those rejecting the worship of the beast are excluded from the social and economic life on earth (13:16) and have to go into captivity and death (13:10). The book of Revelation demands unfaltering resistance to the imperial cult because to give divine honors to Caesar would mean to ratify his claim to power and dominion over all nations and people. The power struggle between the two kingdoms is absolute; no neutral stance is possible.

As the deputies of God's kingdom on earth (1:6; 5:10) the Christians are by definition the enemies of the totalitarian Roman world-empire and its allies. The dwellers of the earth, the free and the slaves, the merchants and the kings of the earth submit to the power of this empire (cf. chap. 17) which corrupts and devastates the earth. The outcries of the Christians for justice and judgment are therefore also on behalf of the earth (6:9; 15:4; 18:20; 20:4–6). God's justice and judgment coincide with human salvation (21:1–7). God's coming in judgment means justice for those who reject the oppression of the great world-power Babylon-Rome which corrupts the earth (19:2). It brings judgment on those who usurped God's and Christ's Lordship over the earth, and liberation for those who have conquered the beast and its image (15:2–4).

Eschatological salvation will mean the destruction of the Roman empire and the idolatrous-dehumanizing forces behind it. In the New Jerusalem God's throne will be among God's people and all dehumanizing and evil powers will be extinguished from the new earth. Those who remained loyal and victorious will reign with God and Christ forever (22:5). In the meanwhile, however, the Christians are still in danger of losing their share in the eschatological reign by giving the emperor honors which belong to God and Christ alone. Such a radical rejection of the Roman power and cult is possible for the Christians because they know that the power of God and Christ will prevail over the anti-divine forces. A victory of God, Christ, and the loyal Christians is at hand and God's reign will soon be reality on earth as it is now in heaven.

Revelation develops in full how the dominion of Christ and God takes hold of the whole world and earth. God's reign is now the reality in heaven, symbolized by God's throne. In the eschatological plagues and in the parousia of Christ it extends to the earth and finally it will destroy all anti-divine powers, death, and underworld. The *first stage* of the gradual extension of God's reign over the whole world is described in broad outlines: In his exaltation Jesus Christ, the slaughtered Lamb, has received the eschatological rule and kingship in heaven. The Lamb was worthy to receive glory and power because he has created a kingly-priestly community of those redeemed from all peoples, tongues, and nations (5:9–10). Jesus Christ is the Lord of the community (1:12–3:21) and of the universe (cf. the plague septets). At the same time Satan is thrown down to earth where he rules through the Roman empire and cult for a short while (chaps. 12–13). The deputies of the kingdom of God and of Satan are therefore pitted against each other in the short time before the End. Even though it appears as if the Christians were losers in this eschatological warfare they are in reality the true victors (cf. chaps. 17–18).

With the parousia of Christ (19:11–16) he *second stage* of the drama has arrived. Christ and the faithful Christians reign as kings over the earth (20:4–6). Babylon-Rome is destroyed, the two beasts are imprisoned, and Satan is thrown into the abyss. All dehumanizing powers, Satan, Death, and Hades are annihilated and all persons are judged according to their works (20:7–15).

The first heaven and the first earth, the dualism between God's and Christ's dominion and that of the devil and Rome, will at a *third stage* give room to a new heaven and a new earth (12:1–22:5). The New Jerusalem, the reality of eschatological salvation and bliss, will come down from heaven to earth and those who have rejected the worship of the beast and its image will reign forever and ever (22:5). The author of Revelation does not envision as Paul did that at the Last Day the Christians "shall be caught up together with them (the dead) in the clouds to meet the Lord" (1 Thess. 4:17), nor does he hope as other apocalyptic writers did that the righteous will become stars in heaven. He sees the New Jerusalem, the holy city of humankind "coming down out of heaven from God" (21:2). The center of the theological movement of Revelation is the earth. True, this new earth will be completely different from the earth and world as we know it. Christ's and God's rule and power will mean the abolishment of all dehumanizing powers and oppressive forces. Not suffering, hunger, captivity, and death, but life, light, and happiness are the characteristic realities of eschatological salvation.

Revelation's concrete vision of eschatological salvation as the nonoppressive power and dominion of God and Christ has not so much moved mainline Christianity as it has inspired messianic and chiliastic movements of all times. Whereas established Christianity has more and more conceived of salvation as spiritual salvation of the soul in the mystic flight out of the conditions of this earth and time, the messianic movements within Christianity have again and again affirmed Revelation's vision of salvation as a concrete earthly reality, as liberation from the oppressive conditions of domination in this world. These movements have always maintained that oppressive political powers and Christian salvation cannot coexist. They have rejected the theological option of established Christianity which maintained that an arrangement and adaption to the present evil political powers is possible for the Christian because they cannot touch the salvation of the soul. Even though the messianic movements of Christianity often assumed a greater active participation of the Christians in the establishment of God's kingdom on earth than the author of Revelation did, they nevertheless hoped with him for the dawn of eschatological salvation on a New Earth in the New Jerusalem freed from all oppressive and dehumanizing anti-divine powers.

This attempt of the author of Revelation to formulate the reality and meaning of eschatological salvation not primarily in spiritualized-religious terms, but in universal-political-human terms gains even greater importance today when many Christians are tempted again to leave the societal-political realm to the anti-divine forces and to seek their salvation in spiritual knowledge and religious experiences. Christians again experience their powerlessness and the temptation to accommodate themselves to the dehumanizing political and societal powers of our time. The book of Revelation encourages us not to dissolve the tension between our everyday experience of powerlessness and our faith conviction that God's healing power of salvation will prevail. With the death and resurrection of Jesus Christ the liberation of God's people has begun. Revelation assures us that we already share in the salvific power of God's dominion. Only by living according to this power and in this power of salvation will we be able to overcome the dehumanizing-oppressive powers of evil in our world.

SELECTED BIBLIOGRAPHIES

HEBREWS

Some of the most important works on Hebrews include the commentary in French by C. Spicq and those in German by H. Windisch and O. Michel. Among German monographs those by Käsemann and Bornkamm are very important. Some of the older commentaries, e.g., Westcott and Moffatt, are still worth reading.

Commentaries:

BRUCE, F. F. *The Epistle of the Hebrews.* (Grand Rapids: Eerdmans, 1964). Bruce is a British conservative Baptist and believes that for Hebrews the sacrifice of Christ is confined to Calvary and that it has no place for a sacrificial interpretation of the eucharist.

BUCHANAN, G. W. *To the Hebrews.* The Anchor Bible 36. (Garden City, N. Y.: Doubleday, 1972). This is by far the most learned of recent commentaries. Its flaw is that, like too many commentaries in this series, it puts forward a highly eccentric view (Christian Zionism).

MONTEFIORE, H. W. *A Commentary on the Epistle to the Hebrews.* Harper-Black Commentaries. (New York: Harper, 1964). A critical-conservative commentary. Montefiore attributes Hebrews to Apollos and dates it before A.D. 70.

Monographs:

BOURKE, M. M. "The Priesthood of Christ," in R. E. Terwilliger and U. T. Holmes, II, (eds), *To Be a Priest,* (New York: Seabury, 1975) pp. 55–69. Bourke champions the affinities of Hebrews with Philo and Platonic thought.

SOWERS, S. O. *The Hermeneutics of Paul and Hebrews. EVZ* (1965). Sowers argues for Hebrews' affinity with Philo.

WILLIAMSON, R. *Philo and the Epistle to the Hebrews.* (Leiden: Brill, 1970). Williamson argues that Hebrews is basically salvation-historical in its dualism.

JAMES

Commentaries:

Aside from some earlier commentaries on James by Mayor (1892), Schlatter (1932), Ropes (1916), Chaine (1927), and Windisch-Preisker (1930), the treatment in *The Jerome Bible Commentary* (1968) should prove helpful.

DIBELIUS, M. (Rev. H. Greeven). *James.* Tr. M. Williams, ed. H. Koester; Hermeneia (Philadelphia: Fortress, 1976).

Articles:

KECK, L. E. "The Poor Among the Saints in Jewish Christianity and Qumran," *ZNW* 57 (1966), 66 ff.

SEITZ, O. J. F. "Relationship of the Shepherd of Hermas to the Epistle of James," *JBL* 63 (1944), 131–140.

SHEPHERD, M. H., JR. "The Epistle of James and the Gospel of Matthew," *JBL* 75 (1956), 40–51.

WARD, R. B. "The Works of Abraham: James 2:14–26," *HTR* 61 (1968), 283–290.

———. "Partiality in the Assembly," *HTR* 62 (1969), 87–97.

1 PETER, 2 PETER, JUDE

Commentaries:

MAYOR, J. B. *The Epistle of St. Jude and the Second Epistle of St. Peter.* (London, 1907, and reprints). An old, but very useful work.

KELLEY, J. N. D. *A Commentary on the Epistles of Peter and Jude.* (New York: Harper and Row, 1969). The best treatment of all three letters available in English.

SELWYN, E. G. *The First Epistle of St. Peter.* (London: Macmillan, 1964). The best commentary on 1 Peter, defending Petrine authorship.

BEARE, F. W. *The First Epistle of Peter.* (Oxford: Blackwell, 2d ed. 1958; 3d ed. 1970). The commentary is pre-form critical and presumes dependence on Pauline letters, but recognizes persecution by the state as background to 4:12 ff.

BEST, E. *1 Peter.* New Century Bible. (London: Oliphants, 1971). A balanced treatment in opposition to Beare and the hypothesis of a baptismal homily.

Monographs and Articles:

DALTON, W. J. "Christ's Proclamation to the Spirits. A Study of 1 Peter 3:18–4:16," *Analecta Biblica* 23. Rome: Pontifical Institute, 1965.

DANKER, F. W. "1 Peter 1:24–2:17, A Consolatory Pericope," *ZNW* 58 (1967), 93–102.

ELLIOTT, J. H. *The Elect and the Holy. An Exegetical Examination of 1 Peter 2:4–10 and the Phrase Basileion Hierateuma.* Suppl. to Nov. Test, vol. 12. (Leiden: Brill, 1966). For a critique see E. Best in *Nov. Test.* 11 (1969), 270–293.

———. "The Rehabilitation of an Exegetical Step-Child: 1 Peter in Recent Research," *JBL* 95 (1976), 243–254. Good bibliography.

BEST, E. "1 Peter and the Gospel Tradition," *NTS* 16 (1970), 95–113.

DANKER, F. W. "2 Peter 3:10 and Psalm of Solomon 17:10," *ZNW* 53 (1962), 82–86.

KÄSEMANN, E. "An Apologia for Primitive Christian Eschatology," in Käsemann, *Essays on New Testament Themes SBT* 41 (London: SCM, 1964), 169–195.

BOOBYER, G. H. "The Indebtedness of 2 Peter to 1 Peter," *New Testament Essays: Studies in Memory of T. W. Manson,* ed. A. J. B. Higgins, (Manchester, 1959), 34–53.

REVELATION

Commentaries:

CHARLES, R. H. *A Critical and Exegetical Commentary on the Revelation of St. John.* 2 vols. (New York: Scribners, 1920). The basic classic commentary.

CAIRD, G. B. *A Commentary on the Revelation of St. John the Divine.* (New York: Harper, 1966).

Monographs:

RISSI, M. The Future of the World, *SBT,* 2d series, 23. (London: SCM, 1972).

FIORENZA, E. S. "The Eschatology and Composition of the Apocalypse," *CBQ* 30 (1968), 537 ff.

———. "Apocalptic and Gnosis in the Book of Revelation and in Paul," *JBL* 92 (1973), 565–581. "Redemptión as Liberation," *CBQ* 36 (1974), 220–232.

HILL, D. "Prophecy and Prophets in the Revelation of St. John," *NTS* 18 401–418.

THOMPSON, L. "Cult and Eschatology in the Apocalypse of John," *Journal of Religion* 49 (1969), 330–350.